Degress with Less Debt

Creative ideas to minimise the cost of your higher education

Jenny Barron, Tamsin Foxwell
and Debbie Steel

Student Helpbook Series

Degrees with Less Debt – Creative ideas to minimise the cost of your higher education

Published by Lifetime Publishing, Mill House, Stallard Street, Trowbridge BA14 8HH

© Nord Anglia Lifetime Development South West Ltd, 2011

ISBN 978-1-904979-47-0

Printed through SS Media Ltd

Cover design by Arthouse Creative

Contents

About the authors

Jenny Barron, Tamsin Foxwell and Debbie Steel are part of the in-house author team at Lifetime Publishing. They contribute to the widely used CLIPS careers information system and have written a range of other student helpbooks and careers resources.

Acknowledgements

The author team would like to thank Helen Evans for her work on this book. We'd also like to take the opportunity to thank Jacki Ciereszko, Norma Evans and Trish Walton for their support behind the scenes.

Introduction

If you are thinking about studying for a degree, the costs involved are likely to be a major consideration. This book aims to offer you some real choices about how, where and what you study – giving you the opportunity to minimise the costs, maximise your income and, therefore, achieve a degree with less debt.

When making decisions about higher education, however, there's more to consider than simply financial matters. The true value of your degree depends on the experiences and opportunities it opens up to you. This book will help you think about what's important to you and how to make sure you get value for money.

Please note

This book is aimed at a UK-wide readership. However, please be aware that some aspects of higher education vary depending on whether you live in England, Wales, Northern Ireland or Scotland – and where you choose to study. Further details are provided as appropriate within the book.

For simplicity, the term 'university' is used throughout the book to describe any institution offering higher education. Therefore, unless otherwise stated, this includes institutions such as further education colleges, distance learning providers and overseas institutions that offer degree courses.

As the book focuses on the ways you can make a difference to the overall cost of your degree, it's important to note that standard student finance arrangements (i.e. student loans, maintenance grants etc) are discussed only briefly.

While every effort has been taken to provide you with accurate information about the options available to you and their financial implications, things do change. You should always check the most up-to-date information available and seek advice as necessary.

Chapter one

Think like an investor

Getting a good education is often described as an investment in your future – and a degree is one of the most highly regarded qualifications you can achieve. If you're thinking about studying for a degree, while you may be tempted to view both the outlay and the reward in purely financial terms, there are also more personal costs and benefits that are worth considering. This chapter aims to help you see beyond just the obvious financial considerations and think instead about how you can maximise the value of your higher education. This chapter will help you:

- understand the investment required and the potential rewards
- decide on the goals that are important to you
- choose your subject wisely
- get more for your money
- think about budgeting
- know what to do if your course doesn't deliver!

The investment – and the rewards

Undertaking a degree course comes at a price. As well as tuition fees and living expenses, you need to take into account the loss of potential earnings while you study. On a personal level, you also need to be committed to investing your time and energy. Studying at degree level can be hard work!

However, there's a great deal of evidence that gaining a degree enriches your life. Not only does it develop your knowledge of your chosen subject, it can also broaden your understanding of the world, help you grow as a person, introduce you to new friends and new experiences and, of course, improve your career prospects! Graduates have a greater range of careers to choose from and studies have found that they tend to find their work more satisfying. It's also been estimated that over the course of a lifetime graduates earn, on average, £100,000 more than non-graduates.

So, if gaining a degree is truly going to be an investment in your future, perhaps you should be thinking like an investor!

What would you do with £30,000?

If you got lucky on the lottery or sold that Ming vase you found in the attic – what would you do with the windfall of cash? While a popular option might be to have a massive party and to blow all the money on having a good time, it wouldn't take too long before the money was spent and you were back at square one. Perhaps a better, or at least a more sensible, option would be to invest the money so that it increases in value and you could ultimately spend it on something much more significant and beneficial.

When you add up the cost of gaining a degree and realise that it could easily amount to £30,000+, you face the same dilemma. Would you spend that amount of money in a completely carefree manner or would you try to maximise the return it could give you? While this book aims to show you ways of reducing the overall cost of your degree, it's safe to say that it's unlikely to be entirely free – so you need every pound of your money to deliver the maximum value possible to you. Which is why you need to think and act like an investor.

Take control

It's easy to become preoccupied with the most obvious costs of your degree – the fees, living expenses and so on. When faced with such large financial undertakings, some people respond by burying their heads in the sand and letting their spending spiral out of control, while other people become overly anxious and end up feeling very negative about their situation. But, while it's natural to worry about taking out loans and running up large debts, it would be a shame to let these concerns ruin your degree experience.

As an investor, you have to take control of your situation and adopt a much more considered approach. It's not enough to make decisions based on costs alone, you also need to factor in the potential benefits of what you will gain from the whole experience. By viewing the cost of your degree as an investment it means that you are far more likely to:

- manage your money

- make decisions objectively

- think about what you are spending every last penny on!

Thinking in this way encourages a positive frame of mind – as you'll be investing in yourself and your future.

Tips for investors

Some important advice for investors is listed below. You'll find these tips are repeated themes throughout this book.

- **Understand the difference between price and value.** While you don't want to spend more than you have to, the cheapest option isn't necessarily the best. Think through the ultimate value you will get from your choices – price is just one consideration.

- **You don't have to follow the crowd.** Your circumstances, goals and values are unique to you, so find the solutions that are best for your situation, even if it means bucking the trend.

- **Do your research.** Take full advantage of all the information out there about subject choices, fees, student satisfaction rates, drop-out rates, bursaries, destinations of previous students and so on. Chapter eight will show you where to find much of this type of information. And make sure you seek advice and guidance if you need it.

- **Trust your instincts.** While it's incredibly important for you to plan and research your options and to get advice, only you will know if your final decision feels right for you. Studying for a degree will seem much easier if you feel committed and enthusiastic from the start, so pay attention to your heart as well as your head.

Whose degree is it anyway?

Perhaps the most important idea to bear in mind, and the one that will influence all the decisions you need to take along the way, is that it is **your** life and **your** degree under discussion. You will be the one having to attend lectures, complete assignments and take exams. When you graduate, you will have all the benefits that come with a degree, but any debt will be in your name – and that debt may well be a part of your life for a considerable period of time.

Make sure that you understand the significance of this, because you'll no doubt be faced with many people who'll have something to say about your choice of subject, university or mode of study. As valuable as their input may be, have the confidence to make your own decisions.

- Your family may have strong views based on their own experiences, but times do change, so make sure you're basing your decision on the most up-to-date information available.

- It may be tempting to copy what your friends are doing – it can be reassuring to know that you're all making similar decisions at such an important time. However, alternative or less obvious choices may work better for you.

- Teachers and careers advisers will be able to give you impartial advice and guidance about your options, but remember that the ultimate decision rests with you.

Decide what's important to you

You will get the most value from your degree if it ultimately helps you get to where you want to be in life. So, take the time to work out what's important to you. Think about what you want from the overall experience; there are various benefits to be gained from a degree, not just the intellectual development that comes from studying a subject at a high level. A degree can:

- open the door to a particular career

- keep your career options open and increase your employability in a number of fields

- provide you with opportunities to gain practical work experience

- help you develop various skills that can increase your employability – from so-called 'soft skills', such as project management and teamwork, to practical skills in languages or ICT, for example

- enable you to move away from home and start fending for yourself in a supportive environment

- offer you the opportunity to study and live abroad for a period of time

- introduce you to a wide range of clubs, societies and activities you might not otherwise have the chance to experience.

Which of these is important to you? This is where understanding the difference between price and value comes into play. Cheaper courses, modes of study or universities may not provide you with the same benefits as other, more expensive options. Having a clear understanding of what you want out of the whole degree experience will help you make objective choices.

Stay focused on your goals

Once you know what it is you are aiming for, make sure you keep those goals at the forefront of your mind. When there are decisions to be made about what, where and how you study, assess your options according to whether they take you a step closer to your goals or not.

This single-minded approach will need to stay with you throughout the duration of your studies. There may be occasions when you find your course difficult or you lose enthusiasm for it; you may feel there are competing pressures on your time or simply more enjoyable things to do than study. Don't be surprised if you feel this way from time to time during your course; you won't be alone. If you are aware from the outset that it won't all be plain sailing, but that your goals are worthwhile and will benefit you in the long run, you are more likely to push through any difficulties.

Choose your subject wisely

One of the key decisions you need to make is which subject (or subjects) you are going to study for your degree. Choosing the right subject for you is perhaps the most important consideration in terms of how much value you will get back from your investment. This is because your subject choice is likely to affect:

- the potential careers open to you once you graduate
- your enjoyment and interest in your studies, which in turn will impact on your motivation and commitment
- your academic results
- the opportunities on offer for developing other useful skills and experience
- whether there is any additional financial support available while you study, such as scholarships, awards or grants.

Chapter two describes the range and type of financial support that you may find available to help minimise the cost of your higher education. While it may be tempting to look for courses that offer the most financial support as your number one priority, when it comes to subject choice, the other factors listed above are just as important to consider, if not more so. As with other decisions that you'll be making, remember to weigh up the potential long-term value of your choices rather than just simply the immediate financial implications.

Think about your potential career opportunities

You'll find that there are some careers that require a degree in a **specific subject** – for example, you need a degree in medicine to become a doctor, a degree in architecture to work as an architect and a degree in modern languages to work as a translator or interpreter. Be aware, also, that for some careers it may be essential or preferable for you to take a course that has been accredited or recognised by a particular professional body.

However, there are many more graduate careers that are flexible in their entry requirements, as illustrated below.

- Some careers are open to graduates with a degree in any **relevant subject** – for example, to work as a meteorologist you may be accepted with a degree in meteorology or in maths, physics, physical geography, computer science etc.

- Some careers require a specific subject at higher education level, which could be a degree in a specific subject **or** a post-graduate qualification gained after a degree in a more general subject – for example, a toxicologist may have specialised in the subject after taking a degree in biology, chemistry, biochemistry, pharmacology etc.

- Many careers are open to graduates with a degree in **any subject** – for example, there are no set subject requirements to start training as a barrister or to work in advertising, housing or stockbroking. Similarly, many management-training schemes and a large number of the roles available through the Civil Service Fast Stream accept graduates with a degree in any subject.

If you haven't already done so, make sure you read up-to-date information or seek reliable advice about careers, before you start making too many decisions. If you have a career in mind that requires a degree in a specific subject, then there is little for you to decide. However, for most people there are choices to be made. Whether you want to keep your career options open or whether there is a variety of subjects that are all acceptable for entry to your preferred career, you need to know that your choices will work out in the long run.

Think about your commitment to your studies

Applying for a subject that interests and motivates you is important for a variety of reasons.

- Even before you start the course, admissions tutors will be looking for evidence of your interest in your subject – and you may not be offered a place without being able to demonstrate your enthusiasm for the topic.

- Once on the course, you will need self-motivation and self-discipline to complete the work required of you. You will be expected to study independently, participate in tutorials, complete group and individual assignments and so on – all so much easier and enjoyable if you feel passionate about the subject!

- Completing a three-year course, or studying for even longer if your chosen course or mode of study requires it, demands a certain amount of stamina. Picking a subject that you enjoy, and that has the potential to keep you interested for the full duration of your course, is going to prove hugely important to your ability to last the distance.

Think about your potential academic results and other achievements

For those careers that are flexible over which subjects are acceptable for entry, you will find that employers place more emphasis on other factors. It's likely that, when faced with large numbers of graduate applicants, employers will consider:

- class of degree – often only short-listing those with an upper second or first class degree

- employability skills – these are the skills that make employees more effective in the workplace, such as skills in ICT, negotiation, languages, communication, leadership, research, commercial awareness, decision making, project management etc

- whether candidates have relevant work experience.

Picking a subject that you believe you will excel in academically and that offers suitable enrichment opportunities, such as the chance to gain employability skills or work experience, is therefore incredibly important and has quite significant implications.

For instance, you may believe that a degree in a work-related subject leads to better career prospects than a more 'academic' subject, but this may not be the case for many careers. As an example of this, consider the scenario of looking for work with one of the well known blue-chip audit firms. You may think that a degree in accountancy and taxation would be your best option. However, in reality, such firms do not specify any particular degree subject for their graduate entry – but do have minimum requirements when it comes to **class of degree** and **personal achievements**.

Therefore, if you know your chosen career is flexible about which subjects are acceptable for entry, you should think about opting for a subject that would enable you to:

- achieve a better class of degree
- gain a broader perspective on the world, which employers may well value
- develop useful skills and experience that enhance your employability.

Think about combined degrees

For some people, there may be a lingering concern that the degree subject that interests them most may be considered too 'academic' or 'arty' for many employers. You may have a strong interest in medieval studies, fine art, English literature or anthropology, for example, but are worried that you would be at a disadvantage when applying for general graduate careers, even with a first or upper second class degree in such a subject.

It's unfortunate, but probably true, that **some** employers believe that these types of subjects don't equip students for the world of work. They may think that studying such subjects won't have enabled you to develop any 'real-world' knowledge or practical skills that would benefit their organisation.

For the reasons given previously, it's important that you pick a subject because you have the potential to do well in it and because it interests you. But if you are really concerned about how potential employers may view your subject, then you could consider taking a combined degree, enabling you to study your preferred subject alongside another subject that could be considered more practical or business orientated.

Universities often offer the opportunity to combine a wide range of subjects. Splitting your course half and half between two subjects is usually known as a joint degree. Alternatively, it is possible to choose major and minor subjects where, for example, your time is split 75% – 25% between the two subjects. You will find a variety of options on offer such as:

- American studies and computing
- biosciences with music
- business management with dance
- business computing and religious studies
- health studies with fine & applied arts.

The benefit of combined degrees is that they allow you to develop a wider knowledge base and greater range of skills than studying a single subject. Another advantage of combined degrees is that they demonstrate that you are versatile and flexible in your approach to your work, useful attributes valued by many potential employers. A well-planned combination of subjects may also help you find employment in niche areas of work that require both commercial skills and specialist knowledge, such as academic publishing, arts administration, sports development work etc.

As always, make sure you do your research before opting for a combined degree, as they aren't for everyone. For example, a single honours degree gives you a greater breadth of knowledge about any given subject than you would get through studying it in combination. You may also find that you have to justify your choices to potential employers if your combination of subjects appears too unrelated.

However, it's also worth remembering that whatever subject or subjects you opt for, it is still possible to:

- sell yourself to a potential employer based on all the transferable skills that you develop through higher education – research, time-management, presentation, communication, teamwork skills etc
- seek out enrichment opportunities while you study (see below), in order to improve your employability.

Get more for your money

Once you are settled on which subject you wish to study, you will be in a position to start comparing different courses at different institutions. Among other considerations, now is the time to start assessing which courses and universities offer the most **'added value'**. This means looking at:

- what opportunities there are to develop transferable skills either through or alongside your studies

- what extracurricular activities are available that will enhance or enrich your university experience

- whether courses offer any optional extras that add to your learning experience and can potentially be a selling point on your CV.

Transferable skills

Most degree courses will help you develop a range of transferable skills, such as teamwork, time management and so on. While employers certainly value these 'soft' skills, they may also look for ability in other, more practical areas, such as languages and ICT.

Check whether you will have the opportunity to develop such skills through:

- course modules that can be taken alongside your main studies

- evening classes, often available at a discounted price

- self-study; for example, through access to a language or IT centre and its resources.

Language skills are obviously useful if you want to work or study abroad, but also if you want to work in the UK for an organisation with international connections. Most universities offer a wide range of modern foreign languages; think about whether developing language skills would benefit you in the future.

Check what opportunities you will have to develop your **ICT skills**, not only in the specific technologies that relate to your field of study, but also in generic applications, such as word processing, spreadsheet, database, presentation, image manipulation and web-related packages.

Find out whether you are likely to be offered help in developing your **research and information-handling skills**. Universities may offer induction sessions that cover how to use the web effectively, perform literature searches and make full use of library resources. Such skills are critical to achieving a degree, but also have many applications in the workplace.

You may be surprised at what else may be on offer – short courses to develop your **enterprise skills**, support your **job search** or help you **get published**; lessons in **touch typing** or **driving**; sessions with **guest speakers** and much more!

Extracurricular activities

The higher education experience needn't just be about studying! There are many clubs and societies you can join at most institutions that can offer a welcome break from academia. Make sure you check out what is on offer before you apply; there may be opportunities to indulge your passions or develop new ones, and on a personal level these may be the things you enjoy most about your time at university.

Such activities may also add significant value to your degree by enhancing your CV in the eyes of a potential employer. Think of all the transferable skills you can gain from being an active member of a sports team, debating society, drama club, music group, college radio station, or student union entertainment team! You'll be able to use this as evidence to potential employers that you are a team player, or even a natural leader, and that you are skilled at organisation, negotiation or promotion, for example. Particularly in the absence of work experience, being able to demonstrate these skills from other areas of your life will be vital when you start applying for jobs. Showing that you have a healthy work-life balance may also be important to some potential employers.

Other available extracurricular options may include joining an **Armed Forces university unit** or undertaking **voluntary work**, the **Duke of Edinburgh's Award** programme, **Young Enterprise Graduate Programme** or other schemes that will enable you to show evidence of personal development.

Optional extras

Depending on the subject that you plan to take, certain courses may provide optional extras that add interest and depth to your studies, as well as helping you develop your skills. Look out for courses that offer:

- field trips – either in the UK or abroad

- behind-the-scene visits to places of interest and relevance to your course

- overseas study placements (see Chapter six for information about spending part or all of your course abroad)

- the chance to meet, network or even undertake short work placements with relevant employers (Chapter three has information about longer work placements, such as a placement years and sandwich courses)

- opportunities to contribute to student- or university-run enterprises.

Some of the optional extras on offer will come at a price. Make sure you know how much you will need to pay and factor this into your cost comparisons of different courses. You will need to judge how much benefit you will gain from the experience, in order to decide whether it is a worthwhile investment.

Look after the pennies...

...and the pounds will look after themselves. Or so the saying goes! While this book doesn't aim to give you lots of money-saving tips along the lines of cutting coupons and growing your own vegetables, you do need to be sure that any money you spend is being invested in things that will benefit you the most and not wasted unnecessarily.

With that in mind, it helps to think about the choices you have about your lifestyle as a student and ways in which you can manage your budget efficiently. Some of the major considerations that will have most impact on your finances are listed below.

- **Living expenses** – your options may include whether you live at home or move away; stay in halls of residence or private accommodation; share grocery bills with fellow students or manage your own shopping and meals etc. Make sure you have taken the time to identify the most cost-effective options for you. Remember to factor in what you will do during vacations, what you will do if halls of residence are not available for the entire course, whether you will need a TV licence, insurance etc.

Chapters five and six look at how your choice of where to study can significantly affect the cost of your higher education.

- **Travel expenses** – these also need to be taken into account when deciding where to study. You will need to factor in the cost of moving yourself and your possessions to your new home, possibly at the start and end of each term. Think also about how you will get to university and back on a daily basis. Running a car costs a lot of money in terms of fuel, insurance, tax, maintenance and repairs. Would a bicycle, moped or public transport be a better option?

- **Study costs** – aside from your fees, make sure you know in advance if there are particular costs associated with your chosen course. You may have to pay for field trips; equipment; professional registration fees; books and resources; photocopying, printing and stationery; etc. Many students supply their own computers, but check out the availability of the university's own IT facilities, which can save you the cost of insurance, battery charging, software, printer cartridges, security packages and broadband. Alternatively you may be able to hire a laptop from the university as and when you need one. Similarly, rather than buying all new books, make good use of the library, or look to buy second-hand books from other students.

- **Leisure time** – the value of extracurricular activities has already been covered, but they may come at a cost, which is worth bearing in mind. However, the main consideration on what you do with your leisure time – evenings, weekends or vacations – is whether you find paid employment. Chapter seven has some advice on student-friendly work options as well as creative ideas on how your leisure interests may earn you money!

Get what you've paid for

Assuming that you've researched your options carefully and started a course that seems like a sound investment, it's crucial that it now delivers exactly what you want, else not only will that research be wasted, but your time and money also. You therefore need to understand what you will be getting for your money and also what to do if this falls short of your expectations.

Student charters

Many universities publish information setting out what you can expect from their courses – and what is expected from you as a student (in terms or participation in lectures, seminars, private study and so on). These are often referred to as student charters, although they may also be known as student agreements, learning partnership agreements, statements of responsibility etc. The Government is keen for all universities to adopt the student charter approach as a way of improving transparency for students.

Student charters typically set out what you can expect in terms of learning support, teaching and research facilities, assessment and feedback, course costs, payment options, employability support, complaints procedures, sporting facilities and so on. In addition, each course is likely to have its own handbook detailing assessment criteria, contact hours, exam arrangements etc.

Though these documents do not normally represent a legally-binding contract between you and the university, they do give you some indication of what to expect from your university experience. Once on a course you really want to see it through to the end, completely satisfied with the whole experience, in order to feel that you have had full value for your money.

Take control of problems

As an investor, it should be fairly obvious that, once you have started incurring the costs associated with a degree, you need to graduate before you can start seeing any return on your investment. If you drop out part way through your studies, you will have spent money but gained very few, if any, benefits.

Only in very exceptional circumstances should you consider cutting your losses and leaving a course. Before you get to that stage, depending on the type of difficulties you are facing, there are certain things you could consider if you are unhappy with how your course is working out. It may be worth knowing about these in advance so that you don't let problems get too serious before taking action.

- You can raise academic matters with your **course leader** or **personal tutor**.

- Speak to the **student rep** for your course if you would prefer not to deal directly with staff yourself. Student reps are elected by their peers to formally represent the student voice in discussions with teaching staff and university management – and can speak on your behalf if you have a grievance or suggestions for improvements.

- Make use of your university's **student welfare services** for help or advice on any emotional or practical matters that may affect your commitment to your course – home sickness, depression, housing issues, financial emergencies and so on. They may be able to offer you access to counselling services, emergency financial support or other types of assistance.

- Get advice from the **Student Union** if you wish to make a complaint about facilities, accommodation etc.

- Be aware that any university you attend will have a **complaints procedure** if informal attempts to resolve problems have been unsuccessful.

- As a final recourse, you have the right to refer complaints to the **Office of the Independent Adjudicator** (OIA), who can review your case if you have a complaint against your university that the internal complaints procedure has been unable to resolve.

So, if you are struggling with your course or are not satisfied with it in any way, take control of the situation and work on resolving the matter. In most cases you will find your university is keen to work with you to sort out problems and help you succeed.

Final thoughts

Hopefully, this chapter has given you a new way of thinking about the value of a degree that will help you base your decisions on more than just the obvious financial costs. As well as deciding what you want from the student experience, you also need to think about how well your degree will serve your ultimate career ambitions – in terms of the subject you choose and the class of degree and employability skills you are likely to achieve. With clear goals in mind, it will be much easier for you to start comparing the different degree courses on offer and finding ways to minimise the cost of your higher education without compromising on those aspects that will make your degree most worthwhile to you.

Ask yourself...

- What are your goals and aspirations?

- Have you chosen a subject you think you will excel at and enjoy?

- What opportunities will you have to enhance your degree studies?

- Have you thought about how you can control cost through your lifestyle choices?

- Do you know exactly what to expect from your university course?

- Are you thinking like an investor?

Chapter two

Get someone else to pay

Why pay more for your university education than you have to? There are organisations out there prepared to help fund your studies. This chapter isn't a complete directory of funding sources, but it will give you an idea of the kind of support that you could receive. It'll look at the extra money – apart from the state funding available to everyone – that could help with the cost of your tuition fees, living expenses and other costs. The chapter covers:

- sponsorships and scholarships from employers, professional bodies and other organisations
- university bursaries, scholarships and other awards
- bursaries for specific courses
- funding from charities and educational trusts
- other initiatives
- things to consider
- how to make a good application.

First things first

You'll find that the terms sponsorships, scholarships, bursaries etc are all used in different ways. Because there's no clear definition of each, there's overlap and inconsistency in the way the terms are used. In this chapter:

- sponsorships and scholarships that are available from employers, professional bodies and other organisations have been grouped together; they are mainly awarded for academic ability

- bursaries and other awards from universities – sometimes also called scholarships –are described separately; they are usually based on your household income, but a range of other criteria can also apply

- funding – often in the form of grants – from charities and educational trusts are grouped together. These are usually only small amounts of money available to certain students.

The information in this chapter is for those who intend to study full time at university. If you're interested in being sponsored to do a degree while working, look at Chapter four. Also, if you are thinking of going to university overseas, scholarships and other funding for this purpose are discussed in Chapter six.

Please note that the examples of scholarships, bursaries, grants etc given in this chapter are available at the time of writing, but you should check their availability and details near the time you need to apply.

Sponsorships and scholarships

Every year, certain employers, professional bodies and other organisations help fund students through their university degree courses.

Most employer-funded sponsorships and scholarships tend to be for those doing courses in engineering, science, technology, business and other vocational subjects. Often schemes are only available for particular courses at named universities. However, there are some schemes where employers are prepared to sponsor you no matter what subject you choose or where you study. For all sponsorships and scholarships, competition is intense.

Employers usually give funding to full-time students who excel academically. This:

- helps to attract the best people to their organisation in the future – this is particularly important where it's hard to find employees with the right skills

- can supply employers with graduates who already know their business and can hit the ground running, as many schemes involve working for the sponsoring organisation during the university vacations.

Apart from through individual employers, there are sponsorship and scholarship schemes run by professional bodies and other organisations.

Once again, they are usually given for academic excellence, but can also be based on other criteria. These schemes are normally aimed at attracting people with potential to a certain profession, such as construction. They may also be used to encourage people from under-represented groups to take up a particular career.

Nowadays, most employers or organisations that offer sponsorship do so for the final year of your degree course only. This might be after you've completed a relevant work placement. However, this isn't always the case and some employers will sponsor you for longer – sometimes for the whole of your course.

Reap the rewards

If you're successful in gaining a sponsorship or scholarship, you may be:

- given a lump sum towards the cost of your studies – you are normally free to do what you like with the cash, but you could use it to help pay for your living expenses while at university; it may mean that you are able to take out a smaller student loan

- formally employed by the sponsoring organisation, receive a salary but attend university full time, as any other student.

The advantages of gaining a sponsorship or scholarship are not just to do with short-term financial gain. Often you get paid work experience in the university vacations, during a gap year before you start your degree course and/or through a sandwich placement. This can mean:

- you will have a chance to find out whether you would be suited to the area of work and the sponsor

- you'll be able to develop your employability skills, such as teamwork

- you'll be ahead of the game when it comes to applying for jobs as you'll already have relevant work experience

- there's usually an offer of employment with the sponsoring organisation when you graduate – in fact, this is normally an expectation.

Examples of sponsorship and scholarship schemes

Armed Forces and Ministry of Defence

All three Armed Forces offer sponsorships to university students, some of which are described below. There are different types of schemes with different levels of commitment – most expect you to take part in relevant university activities and some require you to start officer training when you graduate and then serve a certain number of years.

The **Defence Technical Undergraduate Scheme (DTUS)** is administered jointly by the three Armed Forces and the Ministry of Defence. If you gain a place on an accredited engineering or logistics degree at one of the partner universities, it can pay you £4,000 a year. You have to join a university support unit, undertake regular training and complete paid work placements during the summer vacations. On graduation, you are expected to qualify as an engineering officer and give three years' service.

The **Defence Engineering and Science Group (DESG) Student Sponsorship Scheme** can provide student engineers and scientists enrolled on relevant accredited degree courses an annual bursary of £1,500. You would be required to undertake paid placements during the summer vacation, but unlike the DTUS, there is no commitment on graduation.

For more information on both the DTUS and DESG, see: www.desg.mod.uk.

If you are thinking of training to be a **doctor** or **dentist**, all three Armed Forces offer generous packages of support to the right candidates. For example, the Army will pay your degree course tuition fees and you'll also get an annual salary of around £14,000 for the last three years of your training.

Other types of sponsorships provided by the Armed Forces are described briefly below.

- Regardless of your chosen subject, the **Army** can award you £6,000 if you are doing a three-year degree course, £7,000 for a four-year course and £8,000 for a five-year programme in any recognised subject. You are also paid for the time you spend with your University Officer Training Corps. You must start officer training at Sandhurst before your 29th birthday. For further information on sponsorship schemes in the Army, visit: www.armyjobs.mod.uk/education/grants.

- If you want to become a **Royal Air Force** (RAF) officer in the future, you can apply for the University Air Squadron Bursary of £6,000 split between the second and third years of your degree course. You would be expected to join your nearest University Air Squadron. For more information on sponsorship schemes in the RAF, see: www.raf.mod.uk/altitude.

- The **Royal Navy** also provides university sponsorships for undergraduates with the potential to become officers. Standard Bursaries can provide £1,500 for each year of study on a degree course in any subject. If you take an accredited engineering degree course, Technical Bursaries can give you £4,000 a year while you do your degree. Get more details on sponsorship schemes in the Royal Navy at: www.royalnavy.mod.uk.

For up-to-date and more detailed information on any of the programmes described above, look at the websites given or contact your local Armed Forces Careers Office.

Sponsorship schemes through professional bodies and other organisations

As mentioned earlier in this chapter, there are organisations that offer sponsorships and scholarships in order to promote careers in their areas of interest. A few such schemes are described below; you may be able to find others that apply to you.

ConstructionSkills Inspire Scholarships are for those taking construction-related degrees. They can offer you a grant of up to £6,000, a placement each summer with a sponsoring employer, support from the employer and a chance of a job with the sponsoring organisation when you graduate. You need a minimum of 280 UCAS Tariff points. For more information, see: www.bconstructive.co.uk/inspirescholarship.

QUEST Undergraduate Scholarships are offered through the Institution of Civil Engineers (ICE). In partnership with various civil engineering and construction companies, these offer students on ICE-accredited degrees up to £2,000 a year in financial support, paid work experience opportunities and the potential of graduate employment. Find out more at: www.ice.org.uk/questundergrad.

The Institution of Engineering and Technology (IET) awards a range of scholarships. For information, see: www.theiet.org/scholarships. They include:

- IET Ambition Awards – a scholarship of up to £3,000 a year if you intend to take an IET-accredited degree course and expect to gain at least 300 UCAS Tariff points

- IET Power Academy Scholarships – for students on certain electrical, electronic or power engineering courses. They provide a bursary of up to £2,200 for each year of study, £220 towards the cost of books and software, paid summer work placements and a contribution towards tuition fees if you take up employment with the sponsoring organisation.

Whitworth Scholarship Awards are also available for those who want to study any branch of engineering. You must demonstrate excellent academic and practical skills and the qualities needed to succeed in industry. If successful, you are awarded £4,500 for each year of study for up to four years. For more details, see: www.whitworthscholarships.org.uk.

Individual employer schemes

Lots of companies provide sponsorships. Some take part in the type of schemes described above. Most sponsoring employers provide a very limited number of opportunities each year; a few run bigger schemes. To give you an idea of how employer sponsorship operates in practice, just a handful of schemes are briefly described below.

- **AWE** (a company involved in atomic defence) offers a sponsorship programme for those in the penultimate year of a relevant science or engineering degree course. You apply for a placement year and get paid over £15,000 plus benefits. If you're successful during this time, when you return to university, your tuition fees will be paid, you'll get help with the cost of learning materials and you might even get money towards your living expenses. You can go back to AWE for paid vacation placements and the aim is that you'll work for the company after graduation.

- **Balfour Beatty** (a major infrastructure services business) offers sponsorships for students on particular degree courses at certain universities: civil engineering at Loughborough, Nottingham, Birmingham, Leeds, Southampton, Surrey, Durham; certain construction courses at Loughborough and Salford, and quantity surveying degrees at Northumbria, Nottingham Trent, Loughborough and Liverpool John Moores. For students on other courses, Balfour Beatty also offers industrial placements during university vacations and sandwich years – if you do well on such a placement, it can result in sponsorship. For information visit: www.balfourbeatty.com/graduates.

- A consortium of companies including **Boots**, **Barclays**, **Experian** (a global information services company), **Rolls–Royce**, **Tesco** and **Toyota** are among those that currently offer opportunities to students doing the in-company degree in business management at Nottingham Trent University (NTU). You spend your first year studying full time at NTU and then apply to sponsoring employers. Your second and third years are then spent in the workplace with blocks of university study. Your tuition fees are paid by your sponsoring company and you also get a salary in years two and three. To be accepted on the programme, you'll need at least 340 UCAS Tariff points; you apply through UCAS in the normal way but have to undertake various assessments. For further details, see: www.ntu.ac.uk.

- **Jaguar Land Rover** (the car manufacturer) runs a sponsorship scheme for those studying electrical, electronic or systems engineering. You commit to joining the company every summer for paid vacation placements (and a 12-month industrial placement if appropriate), until you graduate. In return, you get a £1,500 annual bursary for each year of study.

University bursaries, scholarships and other awards

Universities generally use the term 'bursary' for funding based on household income and 'scholarships' for awards based on other factors, such as academic excellence. As mentioned earlier in this chapter, this terminology isn't always clear cut, but in most cases they tend to be:

- non-repayable
- given in cash, but they can be in the form of discounts, e.g. for accommodation or books
- paid in a lump sum, usually at the beginning of your course; sometimes they are paid in instalments.

Universities that charge maximum tuition fees have to provide a minimum level of financial support to students from low-income households. However, you can often get a lot more than this! Some universities are more generous than others, so it's worth doing your homework. Typically, the more selective universities tend to offer higher bursaries. Also, the lower your household income, the more money you may be entitled to. For instance, from 2012, the University of Oxford proposes giving students from households earning less than £16,000 a bursary of £4,300 in their first year and £3,000 each year after that. (Incidentally, Oxford also intends reducing tuition fees for students from low-income households.) At the time of writing, the University's plans have yet to be agreed by the Office for Fair Access (OFFA).

Universities can give additional bursaries, scholarships and other awards for a number of reasons. Find out what you may be entitled to. They may be available to you if you:

- have an excellent academic record (see below)
- are from the local area
- have been in care
- want to take a specific degree course, perhaps where there's a shortage of applicants
- are from an under-represented group.

Examples of university awards based on merit

Lots of universities provide scholarships for outstanding students, but possibly to only one or more per course. The amounts of money involved vary widely. Here are just a few examples:

- the University of East Anglia (UEA) awards scholarships of either £2,000 or £1,000 to chemistry students who make UEA their 'firm' choice before Clearing; for the £2,000 scholarship, students have to get at least grade A in chemistry and AB in two other A level subjects; for the £1,000 scholarship, they need grade A in chemistry and grades BB in their other A level subjects

- the Eliahou Dangoor Scholarship Scheme at the University of Leicester awards entrance scholarships of £1,000 to students in a wide range of mainly science, technology, engineering and mathematics subjects who get at least three grade As in their A levels, or equivalent (the scheme is also offered by other universities, but there may be different criteria)

- the Elizabeth Murray Centenary Scholarship at the University of Birmingham College of Medical and Dental Sciences awards £2,000 a year to students who are going into the second year of a nursing, physiotherapy or social work course who have excelled in the first year; the award is also means tested

- Lyell Bursaries in Earth Sciences at Royal Holloway, University of London provide up to £500 for new earth science students who have achieved 320 or more UCAS Tariff points.

The National Scholarship Programme

From 2012, the National Scholarship Programme (NSP) will be introduced in England. It will allocate funds to universities in order for them to direct money to students from disadvantaged backgrounds. If your family income is less than £25,000, and you fulfil the eligibility criteria set by individual universities, you may be entitled to a one-off package of benefits worth at least £3,000 (pro rata if studying part time). This could be made up of:

- a cash bursary of up to £1,000
- a fee waiver or discount
- free tuition for a foundation year
- reduced cost accommodation.

To find out more, look at university websites. The UCAS website will provide a portal for NSP information in the future.

Sources of information

You can find out more about university bursaries, scholarships and other awards from a number of sources.

- Look at individual university websites or prospectuses.
- The UCAS website, www.ucas.com, has a facility to compare the bursaries and other awards available to you for up to six courses.
- The website www.thecompleteuniversityguide.co.uk has grids that summarise the bursaries, scholarships and other awards available at universities in England, Wales, Northern Ireland and Scotland. Although this is useful for comparison purposes, make sure the information is up to date and reliable.
- The Hotcourses website, www.scholarship-search.org.uk, allows you to search for scholarships and other awards according to institution or subject.
- You could consult the book *University Scholarships, Awards & Bursaries* – published by Trotman, part of Crimson Publishing, £22.99; it describes the range of awards available.
- OFFA and equivalent organisations in other parts of the UK are responsible for ensuring fair access to higher education by students from low-income households and other under-represented groups. Every university has to submit access

agreements explaining what they are doing to encourage fair access. These agreements can give you all kinds of information on bursaries and other types of funding. You can search for funding arrangements at universities in England through: www.offa.org.uk.

In order to work out what you may be entitled to, you can use the student finance calculators on the following websites. If you're from:

- England – www.direct.gov.uk/studentfinance
- Wales – www.studentfinancewales.co.uk
- Northern Ireland – www.studentfinanceni.co.uk
- Scotland – www.saas.gov.uk.

Bursaries for specific courses

NHS Student Bursaries

At the time of writing, decisions about funding arrangements for students doing professional healthcare courses from 2012 have yet to be published, so it's important to check what you may be entitled to nearer the time.

The following information applies to students who gain NHS-funded places in England starting in the year 2011/12.

- Income-assessed NHS Bursaries are available for pre-registration degree courses in a number of healthcare professions such as dental therapy, nursing, occupational therapy, physiotherapy and radiography.
- NHS Bursaries are also available for students doing diploma courses in nursing and operating department practice; these are not dependent on your household income.
- Medical and dentistry students can apply for income-assessed NHS Bursaries in the later stages of their training.

In addition to the NHS Bursaries listed above, your tuition fees are normally paid and, in certain circumstances, you may be eligible to receive additional allowances. Depending on your course, you may also be entitled to apply for a maintenance loan.

If your place isn't funded by the NHS, you will be subject to the same financial arrangements as other undergraduates.

Similar arrangements apply across the UK, but there are variations. Funding is administered by different authorities. For more information, consult the relevant authority:

- in England, tel: 0845 358 6655 or see: www.nhsbsa.nhs.uk/students

- in Wales, tel: 029 2019 6167, or view: www.nhswalescareers.com

- in Northern Ireland, tel: 028 9025 7777, or view: www.delni.gov.uk

- in Scotland, tel: 0845 111 1711, or find information on: www.saas.gov.uk.

Social Work Bursaries

If you take an approved degree in social work, you may be able to apply for a non-income-assessed Social Work Bursary or similar grant. Each country in the UK administers financial support for its own residents. Social Work Bursaries are under review, so check whether they are available and, if so, how much you will get. For information, contact the relevant authority or view their websites:

- if you're from England, tel: 0845 610 1122, or see: www.nhsbsa.nhs.uk/swb

- students from Wales should see: www.ccwales.org.uk/social-work-students

- if you're from Northern Ireland, contact your local Education and Library Board.

Funding for teacher training courses

Bursaries for teacher training are only available for those doing postgraduate courses. However, if you do an undergraduate degree to train to teach a secondary priority subject in Wales, you may be eligible for a grant during your school-based placement. Also, extra support may be provided if you train to teach through the medium of Welsh. Further information is available from initial teacher training providers by calling the Teaching Information Line on 0800 389 2500 (or 0800 085 0971 for Welsh speakers) or through: www.tda.gov.uk.

Funding from charities and trusts

There are hundreds of educational charities and grant-making trusts through which it may be possible to get some help towards paying for your studies. The amount of money you get from this kind of source is usually quite small and would be unlikely to pay for your whole course. But remember that every little helps! The funding may be available either as a loan to be repaid after your course or (more likely) as a non-repayable grant.

Are you likely to be eligible?

Many funds are only available for specific students, such as those who:

- are from a certain area of the country
- belong to a particular minority ethnic group
- are female
- have a disability
- come from a low-income household or who are in particular financial need
- have been in care
- went to a particular school
- intend to study a certain subject
- have or had a parent or even a grandparent who followed a particular occupation!

As you can see from the examples given below, some are only available for students who fulfil more than one of the criteria listed above.

Charities and trusts will want to make sure that you have good reason to be given support, so you normally have to give detailed information so that they can make a decision. You will need to do careful research and make sure you understand all the eligibility criteria.

Examples of grants

Many grants are from individual philanthropists, grateful alumni, community groups and so on. Some grants are only available if you can't get funding from elsewhere. Here is a small selection:

- Association of Professional Foresters Education and Provident Fund – for members and children of members of the Forestry and Timber Association – awards one-off grants of up to £500 towards course fees or excursion costs

- The Belfast Association for the Blind – for people in Northern Ireland who are registered blind – grants of between £250 to £350 are awarded for course fees, computers etc

- The Foundation of St Matthias – for students studying in accordance with the doctrine of the Church of England, preferably those living in the dioceses of Bath & Wells, Bristol and Gloucester; can provide one-off grants of up to £750 to help pay for tuition fees, books, living expenses or study abroad

- Joseph Boaz Charity – people from Hull and East Yorkshire can apply for grants of between £250 and £500 to help pay for books, equipment and instruments

- The Leverhulme Trade Charities Trust – provides bursaries to relatives of commercial travellers, chemists or grocers

- Lionel Bart Foundation – drama students can apply for one-off grants of between £1,000 and £3,000

- The Macfarlane Walker Trust – for music students who are in financial need – preferably those from Gloucestershire – can provide grants of between £500 and £2,000 to help buy instruments and other equipment

- Sir John Sumner's Trust – for students studying nursing, medicine or veterinary science who are in need; preference is given for those living in the Midlands; provides grants towards equipment, instruments, fees or living expenses

- The South Square Trust – for students studying the applied or fine arts, particularly practical courses in gold, silver and metal work – can issue one-off grants of over £500

- The Tasker Milward and Picton Charity – for former pupils of certain schools in Haverfordwest, Pembrokeshire, who are experiencing financial hardship or other circumstances that could affect their studies; can provide both one-off and recurrent grants ranging from £100 to £1,000. Grants can be used to pay for books, living expenses or study overseas.

Find out more

The following books published by the Directory of Social Change list possible sources of non-statutory funding. Make sure you consult the latest editions; they should be available for reference in libraries:

- *The Guide to Educational Grants* – lists sources of help for students in financial need
- *The Guide to Grants for Individuals in Need* – lists sources of help for anyone suffering poverty.

The Uni Grants website, www.unigrants.co.uk, allows you to search for grants by location or course and subject.

The Educational Grants Advisory Service (EGAS) operates an online grants search tool, see: www.family-action.org.uk/educationalgrantssearch.

Other initiatives to help you reduce your debt

Apart from all the various sponsorships, scholarships, bursaries, grants and other awards mentioned in this chapter, there are an increasing number of other initiatives to help students and graduates reduce their debt. To attract the best graduates, some employers are willing to pay off some or all of your tuition fee loan after you graduate, for instance. Even the Government is considering paying off student loans for those who train to teach shortage subjects in England.

The one downside worth considering is that there's no guarantee that you'll be successful in your application for these types of initiatives – and you won't know for sure until after you have graduated and paid out. However, while you study, it's worth keeping your eyes open for such schemes. You may be able to start developing a relationship with an employer through vacation work, or similar, that'll put you in a stronger position when it comes to applying after you graduate.

There may be more initiatives being set up in the future, so it's worth looking out for them. Here are a couple of specific examples.

The pharmaceutical company **GlaxoSmithKline** is willing to pay back up to £27,000 in tuition fees for 50 to 100 of its best graduate trainees. In return, the trainees have to stay at the company for a number of years after the fees have been repaid. The scheme is for scientists, chemists and pharmacists, as well as for lawyers, economists and other top graduates.

For a degree with a real difference, **KPMG** (a leading provider of accountancy services) will pay £20,000 a year salary, the tuition fees and accommodation costs of selected accountancy students at Durham University. You have to sign a six-year contract. For the first four years you split your time between university and KPMG's London offices. You are then guaranteed two years' work ending with a salary of £45,000 a year. KPMG is keen to recruit young people from disadvantaged backgrounds and is planning on expanding the scheme to other universities. Meanwhile, Durham University is in negotiation with other major employers to run similar programmes.

Things to think about

Does all this sounds too good to be true? Hopefully not! Organisations have different requirements, and you will want to find a source of funding and a course that are right for you. Depending on you and your situation, there could be some possible drawbacks. Most of these can be overcome, or may not matter to you, but you need to be aware of them nevertheless.

- Remember that competition for certain types of funding, such as sponsorships, can be intense.

- Think about whether you meet all the necessary criteria.

- If you look for a course based purely on the chance that you may get financial support, this may limit your choice of subjects.

- If the funding is for a vocational course, such as engineering or medicine, you may find yourself committing to a career decision before you are fully ready. Think about your future career aims very carefully before you apply for funding.

- You may have to make some kind of commitment to the organisation that funds you. For example, they may expect you to work for them during every summer vacation – this would give you little time to do other things, such as travel. Also, some sponsoring employers expect you to work for them for at least a year after you finish university. This might seem fine now, but will you feel the same when you graduate?

- Make sure you know what your obligations will be.

- Are you sure that you won't have to pay back any money you receive? Most of the sources of funds described in this chapter are not loans and don't have to be repaid, but do double check.

- Some awards (e.g. through the Armed Forces) may be subject to repayment if you change your mind or fail the course.

Making a good application

The way in which some funds are awarded can be pretty complicated. You probably feel that you have enough on your plate, but time spent researching possible sources of finance and putting in a good application will be time well spent.

How you should apply will vary depending on the funding opportunity, so check out what's expected. Here are some general tips:

- double check that you meet all the eligibility criteria otherwise you'll be wasting your time; if you are unsure, contact the organisation concerned

- read any guidance notes very carefully

- find out the best time to apply – for certain types of awards, you may have to apply as much as 18 months in advance

- tailor your application to appropriate organisations; it's far better to a send a few, high-quality applications than lots of rushed, mediocre ones

- apply for university through UCAS in the usual way; don't delay your application just because a sponsorship or other award hasn't been finalised

- if a sponsoring employer expects you to complete a year's work placement with them before you start university, you may have to apply for deferred university entry.

Final thoughts

With rising tuition fees, it's more important than ever that you find out whether someone else would be prepared to help fund your university studies. Some awards can provide you with considerable financial support. But, no matter how small, it's worth claiming everything you're entitled to – even a tiny amount can go a long way to cover your study or travel costs, for instance. Use the various sources of information outlined in this chapter to research what's available.

Ask yourself...

- Are there any employers you'd like to work for who may be prepared to sponsor you?

- What bursaries and other awards are provided by the universities you're interested in?

- Are there any grants you could access to pay for things like books or equipment?

- Do you fulfil all the eligibility criteria for the funding you are considering?

- Have you explored every possibility?

Degrees with Less Debt

Chapter three

Take a different route

Did you know that there are lots of different full-time routes you could take to get a degree that may work out cheaper than the traditional university route? This chapter will look at all the alternative routes, including:

- courses at further education (FE) colleges

- accelerated courses

- learning in stages

- sandwich degree courses.

Although you need to look at every way of keeping your debt as low as you can, you also need to bear in mind that the course you choose still needs to be right for you. Making the wrong choice and dropping out because your course doesn't suit you will end up costing you money and setting back your career plans. Don't underestimate how important it is that the choice you make is right for you, not just your bank account!

What are your options?

If you feel like a full-time course is really the best option for you, then it's worth looking at the different types of full-time courses and education providers available. If you've always assumed going to a university for three years is the best way to go, think again. A further education college or an accelerated course may well be able to offer you the course and qualification you want – at a more affordable price.

Courses at further education colleges

Living at home and studying at your local FE college is one option that may be open to you. There are over 260 FE colleges in the UK that offer higher education (HE) qualifications, such as degrees. Some have the power to award qualifications themselves but many are linked with nearby universities, which validate the programmes they offer.

Around 170,000 students are currently studying for an HE qualification at an FE college. This number has increased in the past few years, and on closer inspection it's not hard to see why.

The benefits of living at home and studying at your local FE college include:

- reduced costs
- less upheaval – you won't have to get to know a new area
- you'll be able to keep any part-time jobs you have
- you can continue any hobbies or local commitments you have, such as playing in a local sports team
- many FE colleges have links with local employers, and some even run their own business such as a recruitment agency, farm, restaurant or garden centre. This might not sound important now, but these links can make your life much easier if you're looking to get useful work experience during your studies.

Many people choose to study at their local FE college as they want to stay close to family and friends.

One of the attractions of studying at an FE college is the reduced cost, but to make a saving, you'll need to do your research and look at tuition fees and your living costs.

Fees

Tuition fees at FE colleges vary considerably. While, at the time of writing, some do charge the same rates as universities, others have significantly lower fees (either overall or for the second and third years of a course). According to recent research (April 2011) conducted by the Association of Colleges (AoC), the majority of colleges are planning to charge fees of less than £6,000 from 2012/13.

If there are a few FE colleges near you it's worth doing your research, as prices may well vary.

Living costs

If your local FE college charges the same for a course as the university you had in mind, you may not see the point of even considering the FE college.

But the cost of a degree isn't just the fees. If you move away from home you'll have to pay for accommodation, food, travel and perhaps utilities, all of which add up very quickly. Research by the AoC (conducted in 2010) found that students who graduate from FE colleges have, on average, around £17,500 less debt than university graduates. The AoC also found that the average cost of studying at an FE college, including fees, travel costs, living expenses and study materials was £8,967 per year in 2010.

If living at home is an option for you, you will need to discuss things with your family before you make any decisions. They may well expect some kind of contribution for rent/food. One of the big draws of staying at home is the reduced cost – but don't assume you'll get away with paying nothing! Chapter five has more information on living at home while you study.

What's available?

The range of HE courses on offer at FE colleges varies, and this may well affect whether this is a viable option for you. Some FE colleges have thousands of students and an impressive range of courses, from electrical engineering to contemporary dance. Some, however, have a much smaller range.

Three-year, full-time degree courses are available at a number of FE colleges. However, colleges that run HE courses nearly always offer foundation degrees and Higher National Diplomas (HNDs). A few FE colleges offer courses leading to a Diploma of Higher Education (DipHE). You may not be as familiar with these qualifications and if this is the case don't dismiss them, they are recognised HE-level qualifications that can lead to a degree.

Foundation degrees are roughly equivalent to the first two years of an honours degree. They are available in work-related subjects and are designed with the help of employers to make them relevant to the workplace. Although lots of people study for foundation degrees on a part-time basis, many full-time courses are available; they usually take two years to complete.

HNDs are also available in work-related subjects and aim to prepare the student for a particular area of work. HNDs take two years to complete on a full-time basis.

DipHEs are available in work-related subjects and are required for certain careers, such as operating department practice. They are equivalent to the first two years of an honours degree and take two years of full-time study to complete. The number of DipHE courses has been reducing in recent years, but they are still a valid qualification.

Foundation degrees, HNDs and DipHEs can all be 'topped up' to a degree with a further year's study. FE colleges often have arrangements with the university that validates their qualifications, allowing students who complete an HND or foundation degree to transfer onto the third year of a degree course at the validating university.

Many colleges don't allow students to enrol for a three year, full-time degree course from the outset. Instead, students have to complete a foundation degree or HND and only then are they offered the chance to 'top-up' their qualification to a degree. This would not make any difference to the qualification you achieve; you would still have a degree and it would still take three years, full time, to complete. Gaining a degree in stages is also discussed later in this chapter.

As stated earlier, foundation degrees, HNDs and DipHEs are only available in work-related subjects, so they may not be an option for you if you intend to study a purely academic subject, such as physics. However, if you haven't decided exactly what you'd like to study, it's worth checking out what your local FE college has on offer. See their website or prospectus for details and find out whether any courses that interest you have 'top-up' routes.

What's it like to study at an FE college?

To help you decide whether or not studying at an FE college is for you, you'll need to find out a bit more about the college and their student experience. In general, studying for an HE qualification at an FE college is a very different experience to university. FE colleges are usually smaller than universities, this means:

- class sizes are smaller
- there may be more contact with tutors and lecturers
- there may be less going on socially; universities usually run lots of different societies, club nights etc that students can take part in; FE colleges don't normally offer students such a wide range of social activities
- you may not have access to the same facilities as you would at a larger university, although this isn't always the case

- the lecturers will not be as involved in academic research compared to those based at a university

- there will be younger students around, who are aged 16-18.

FE colleges and universities both offer different experiences, but one isn't better than the other. What's important is that the experience you choose is one that **you** will enjoy. For some people, FE college offers a route to a degree that isn't as daunting as going away to university, but for others the experience isn't what they expect and want from their time in higher education.

Accelerated courses

If you want to study full time but the cost of a three-year degree course seems too much, you could consider taking an accelerated degree course. These courses take two years, full time but still lead to a degree. Instead of a long summer break, students continue studying and cover the same amount of work as on a three-year course, just over a shorter period of time.

Accelerated courses can save you money. By studying for two years rather than three, you can avoid paying for one year's tuition and a year's worth of living costs (accommodation, food, travel etc). However, you should bear in mind that an accelerated course will be more intensive and allow you less time for paid work, which many students rely on to bring in some extra cash.

At the moment, there are not many universities offering accelerated courses, but in the future this may change as many students look for courses that provide the best value. MPs have also commented that accelerated courses may well become the logical choice for many students.

Currently, the leading provider of accelerated degree courses is the University of Buckingham, the only independent university in the UK. All their undergraduate degree programmes are available as two-year, accelerated courses. For more information, or to search for courses, see: www.buckingham.ac.uk.

BPP University College offers two-year, accelerated degree courses in professional accounting and in business studies. It also runs an accelerated LLB law degree. BPP has campuses in London and Manchester. More information about their courses can be found on: http://undergraduate.bpp.com.

The SAE Institute, Oxford, offers a number of courses in creative media, including two-year accelerated degree courses in film making and audio engineering. SAE is also a private provider. For more information see: www.oxford.sae.edu.

The College of Law has recently announced that it will offer a two-year accelerated LLB law degree from September 2012. Courses will run in Chester, Birmingham and London. More information will be available on: www.college-of-law.co.uk.

As other accelerated courses are likely to be available in future, it's worth looking for courses that are run on this basis when you are researching your options. The results from the course search facility on the UCAS website can tell you whether or not the degree programmes you're looking at take two or three years to complete. For details, see: www.ucas.com.

N.B. Check out the tuition fees for private institutions carefully. Some may charge more per year than publicly-funded institutions. However bear in mind that you would be paying for two years' fees rather than three.

Learning in stages

It goes without saying that one of the major expenses you will encounter as a student is tuition fees. Although there are loans for fees, which mean you don't have to fork out the money up-front, you will have to pay them back eventually. Your other major costs are living expenses (accommodation, food, travel etc), which can mount up quickly. Three years of full-time study means you will be faced with these costs continually and even with the government financial help that is available you're likely to get into debt. But, don't panic, you can avoid some of this debt by learning in stages, allowing you to earn and save towards your next stage.

To avoid debt, you need to earn money. To earn useful amounts of money that will pay your costs while you study, you need to work. But to work, you need time away from study! Does this sound like an impossible situation to you? If so, there is an answer.

This section of the chapter will explore the following options that can provide you with the time you need to boost your earning power:

- taking an alternative route to a degree
- following a sandwich degree.

Taking an alternative route to a degree

Although taking a three-year degree course is the usual way to achieve a degree, it isn't the only way. As discussed earlier in this chapter, foundation degrees, HNDs and DipHEs are HE qualifications in their own right, but can also be used as stepping stones to achieving a degree.

Foundation degrees, HNDs and DipHEs can be studied on a full-time basis, over two years. Many people achieve them and then stop studying and start their career. But lots of people complete another year's study to 'top-up' to a full degree.

To spread the cost of your studying and therefore allow yourself time to earn money to support yourself, you could follow a two-year, full-time course, leading to either a foundation degree, HND or DipHE. You could then take a year (or longer) out to work and save money, before starting another year of study to top up your qualification to an honours degree. Gaining a degree in this way makes absolutely no difference to the value of your final qualification.

During the break in your studies, you ideally need to find a job that:

- earns you money

- helps you develop useful skills that you will be able to use again

- provides you with relevant, workplace experience in the sector you are interested in.

As you will already have an HE qualification, you will be of interest to prospective employers and will be able to apply for a greater range of jobs than those students on a gap year before university. Think about the career you are interested in and consider all the opportunities open to you. You may not yet have the qualification you need to get the exact job you want, but is there a more junior role you could apply for? Most organisations employ administrators and other support staff.

You may even find a job with an employer who is willing to fund your final year at university, perhaps allowing you to study on a part-time basis. See Chapter four for more information on employer-funded study.

Would this be possible for the subject you're interested in?

Taking the route described above isn't possible for some careers, as foundation degrees, HNDs and DipHEs generally relate to a particular area of work, so they aren't available in all subject areas. However, more and more universities are running foundation degrees and the range of subjects is increasing. Examples of current foundation degree courses include: marine engineering, environmental health, finance and law, forensic science and history, heritage and archaeology.

You can search for full-time foundation degree, HND and DipHE courses on the UCAS website, www.ucas.com. When you're looking at courses it's a good idea to check if the university/college has a top-up programme that you can apply for at a later date. However, you don't necessarily need to attend the same university/college to complete your top-up year.

If you have a particular career in mind, it's always best to check the acceptability of the courses you are interested in, before committing yourself. Some careers require applicants to have completed accredited or recognised degree courses – if this is the case for the area of work you are interested in, it's particularly important to do your research first. Speak to the careers adviser at your school or college or the relevant professional body for the career you're interested in.

Is it worth the hassle?

In a word, yes. By choosing to achieve your qualification in stages you will be able to have a break after two years and put off further study until it is a financially-viable option for you. It's worth remembering that you will have achieved an HE qualification, so more demanding and better-paid roles will be open to you at that stage.

Any money that you earn during your time out could be used to:

- help pay off any debts you've accumulated during your first two years of study

- pay for tuition fees in your final year

- pay for accommodation or living costs in your final year.

Sandwich degrees

You've probably heard of sandwich degrees, but did you know that they can help you earn money while you gain valuable work experience?

Sandwich courses typically last four years and combine full-time study with one or more industrial placements, i.e. supervised, practical experience and training with an employer. Many sandwich courses involve spending a whole year in the workplace – this year is sometimes referred to as a placement year. To find out if there are sandwich courses in the subject you want to study, use the UCAS website to search for courses by attendance type.

Sandwich courses that include a paid year in industry can be a way of reducing your debt as you'll have an income for a year. You may be able to use the money you've earned to help pay off any debts or you might be able to put money aside to support yourself during your final year at university. How much you'll earn depends on your placement, but, as an example, Aston University reports that, on average, their students earn £15,000 during their placement year.

Do your sums

Although a sandwich course can be a way of earning while learning, they can cost you money too. Before you commit yourself to a sandwich course, there are a few things you should find out first.

How much will your university charge you for tuition during for the placement year? Even though you won't actually be at university, you'll probably have to pay tuition fees for your placement year. You aren't completely independent of your university during your time at work; staff offer students support while they are on their placement (they may visit you) and may require you to submit work for assessment. Fees for placement years vary from university to university, some only charge a few hundred pounds and others charge up to 50% of a year's tuition.

Will your placement be paid and, if so, how much? Many placements are paid – however, many language students can choose to spend their placement year studying at a university abroad, which obviously wouldn't earn you any money.

How much will it cost you to do the placement? You will have to support yourself during your placement year. You will need to pay for your accommodation, living expenses and travel costs using anything you earn, before you can put any money aside for your final year. It's a good idea to look at your budget and work out how much you'll need to earn to cover your costs and how much you'll be able to save.

Ask questions

If you think a sandwich degree could be an option for you, look into how closely connected your university is with key employers in the industry and how much help you will receive in finding placements. Find out where students have been placed before.

Final thoughts

This chapter has shown you that a traditional, three-year course at a university isn't the only full-time route to a degree; there are other options that can save you money. You don't have to follow the crowd and do what everyone else is doing; perhaps an alternative route would suit you and your budget better. If the ideas in this chapter have sparked your interest, do you own research and find out what's available.

Ask yourself...

- Would you enjoy studying at your local FE college?

- Would you feel you've missed out if you went to an FE college rather than a university?

- Would you be prepared to learn in stages?

Chapter four

Work your way through your degree

If you're keen to spread the cost of studying and want to work a few more hours to avoid borrowing money, then a part-time degree course could be the way forward for you! A lot of people choose to study for their degree on this basis; in fact, around 40% of current undergraduates are following part-time courses. This chapter will look at the various ways you could study part time, including:

- courses at further education (FE) colleges and universities
- distance-learning courses
- employer-funded study and Higher Apprenticeships.

The benefits of studying part time

Studying part time can help you keep your debt as low as possible. By studying part time rather than full time you'll also be able to work more hours and therefore earn more money. Obviously, the more you earn, the less you'll have to borrow.

Apart from earning money, there are other benefits to working and studying part time, including the following.

- **Gaining experience.** All jobs can offer you the chance to learn new skills, and by combining work and study you'll be learning new skills and getting valuable workplace experience while you work towards your degree!

- **Applying what you're learning in a real-life context.** If you can find work related to the subject that you're studying, not only will it look good on your CV, it'll also give you the chance to relate the topics you're studying to real-life situations.

- **It shows commitment!** Juggling the demands of studying and a job can be hard, but it will certainly impress any future employer. Studying and working shows that you are motivated, able to organise your time and can manage different tasks – these are all strengths that employers value.

There are two main ways of studying part time. You could enrol for a course at a university or FE college and attend a campus (perhaps in the evenings) or you could study at home through distance learning. Both of these options have their advantages but you will need to choose a route that suits your learning style and time constraints. For example, courses run on a distance-learning basis are entirely dependent on self-directed learning – you will have to decide when to study as no one will be monitoring you! If you enjoy learning at your own pace, at a time convenient to you, then a distance-learning course may be the right choice. However, if you prefer to have regular face-to-face contact with tutors and other students, courses that involve spending time at a college or university, attending lectures and seminars may well be a better option for you.

Part-time courses at universities and colleges

The majority of universities and many FE colleges offer degree courses on a part-time basis. There is a huge range of courses available. If you don't know much about part-time degree courses, then this part of the chapter might just surprise you; colleges and universities are offering all sorts of ways for students to continue their learning and manage other commitments, such as work.

How long is it going to take?

Part-time courses are usually designed to be flexible. Universities and colleges recognise that many students have to fit their studies around other commitments, such as work and family, so they generally allow you to study at your own pace.

Most courses are made up of modules, with each attracting a certain number of credits. To get your degree you will need to achieve a specific number of credits. On some courses, modules are all worth the same number of credits. However some courses include double modules, worth double the number of credits. The sooner you achieve the required number of credits, the sooner you graduate! The majority of part-time courses allow students to choose how many modules to study per term (there is usually a minimum and a maximum).

How long it will take you to complete your degree will depend on how much studying you are prepared to take on at once. It is possible to complete a part-time degree course in four years; some universities however, allow you to spread your studying across up to ten years!

How are courses taught?

How part-time courses are taught varies and you will need to check out prospectuses and websites, and talk to the colleges/universities you are interested in to find out exactly what they offer. You might:

- attend lectures and seminars during the day, alongside full-time students

- go to classes during the evening, perhaps one or two nights a week

- take part in workshops or lectures at the weekend

- do a mixture of all of these things and possibly do some of your work online.

All these methods of delivery have their advantages, but some may suit your needs more than others. For example, an evening course could allow you to get a job during the day – and would leave your weekends free for independent study and some down time. A daytime course, however, might be more appropriate for you if you want to feel part of everyday campus life and get a job during the evenings.

What's available?

The range of courses on offer to you depends on whether you are looking to stay at home during your course, or move away. As discussed in Chapter five, choosing to live at home could save you a lot of money!

Part-time courses are becoming more popular. Many universities offer a huge range of part-time courses and some even specialise in them!

Birkbeck College in London, for example, is a specialist provider of higher education (HE) courses that are run in the evenings.

As you probably already know, if you're trying to find a full-time degree course then the UCAS website, www.ucas.com, has a search facility that makes it much easier to see the range of courses on offer. Unfortunately though, UCAS doesn't currently list part-time courses, but there are several ways you can find out what's on offer.

- Check out the websites of universities and colleges you're interested in (perhaps the ones nearest you) – most have simple course search facilities that allow you to specify if you are looking for a full- or part-time course.

- If you're looking to attend a college or university nearby, why not go along to an open event or make an appointment to discuss your options? All institutions welcome enquiries from prospective students.

- The Hotcourses website, www.hotcourses.com, has a section dedicated to part-time courses that allows you to search for degree courses in the subject of your choice. You can also search for courses run during the day or evening.

Not sure it's for you?

Studying part-time doesn't suit everyone and if you're not sure if it's for you, then you need to do some more research. Most colleges and universities have open days that are a great way of finding out a bit more about the institution and can give you a real feel for the place and whether it would suit you. Open days also offer you the chance to meet current students – some of whom may be studying on a part-time basis. Speak to students and the university/college admissions staff, and be honest about any concerns you have.

Things to find out

You've chosen the college or university, you've found the course for you and you're ready to go. But, before you apply for the delights of HE, you'll need to do a bit of research first.

Check out what financial support is available to you

The availability of non-repayable funding varies so check out whether your college or university offers any bursaries or grants for part-time students.

Find out college/university application deadlines

Unlike applications for full-time courses (which are through UCAS) applications for part-time courses have to be submitted directly to the college or university you are applying for. Start dates for courses vary, so find out when your application has to be in.

Ask whether the timetable will change

If you are planning to find paid work during your course you will need to know when you are expected to attend college/university and whether this is likely to change as the course progresses.

Distance-learning courses

Distance learning, sometimes referred to as open learning, e-learning or self study, involves working towards a qualification remotely – i.e. not attending a university or college on a regular basis. The flexibility and cost-saving benefits that distance learning offers to students may well be reasons why it has become so popular in recent years. For example, in 2008/09 the number of 18-year-olds who applied to study with the Open University (OU) increased by 17% from the previous year.

Although the majority of distance-learning students choose to combine part-time study with employment, it is also possible to study for a degree through distance learning on a full-time basis.

Distance-learning might be an option for you, if:

- you enjoy learning on your own, but like to know you have support if you need it
- you can't always study on the same days or at the same times each week
- you are motivated and prefer independent study
- you enjoy learning at your own pace
- you don't live within travelling distance of an FE college or university
- you don't want to move away but the course you want to do isn't offered in your area.

How much does distance learning cost?

Fees for distance-learning courses vary. Many providers calculate the cost of programmes by charging per module. Some offer the chance to pay by instalments, which means you can spread the cost and perhaps avoid taking out a loan.

In general, tuition fees are less than those for a traditional campus-based course. Distance-learning courses aren't cheap – you are still paying for HE-level tuition – but it is definitely possible to save money when compared to what you could pay on a full-time, campus-based course. The OU gives examples of course costs on its website, www.open.ac.uk, a psychology degree, for example, studied part time over six years, including all assessments and learning materials, costs in total £4,980 (February 2011). At the time of writing many distance-learning providers have reported that their fees are likely to increase in the coming year, however, it's very unlikely that they will match those charged for many campus-based courses.

By choosing to study by distance learning you can instantly save money in other ways too. You won't have travel costs, for example. If you're able to continue living at home while you study, you'll also be able to save money on accommodation and living costs – don't underestimate how much this could save you, it could amount to thousands of pounds!

The easiest way to avoid debt as a student is to combine your studying with paid work. The advantage of distance learning is that you don't have to study at specific times. As long as you get the work done, it doesn't matter if you study in the morning, evening or at weekends; whereas on a course requiring attendance at lectures, seminars etc you will have to attend at particular times. This flexibility makes it much easier to balance study with paid work, and the more you earn, the less you'll need to borrow!

How would you learn?

Courses are delivered in different ways, but may involve:

- using books, journals and other written materials
- watching TV programmes or DVDs online
- downloading lectures as podcasts
- completing experiments using kits you receive through the post
- watching lectures through videoconferences or webcasts
- taking part in webinars (a seminar conducted over the internet) and interacting with tutors and fellow students.

Some distance-learning degree programmes include week-long residential courses, which involve working with other students or, if your course calls for it, experiments or practical work that you can't carry out at home. Many courses also offer you the chance to attend tutorial sessions occasionally, so you can meet you tutors face to face and discuss your work with them.

The work involved in a distance-learning degree course is no different to what would be expected of you on a traditional campus-based course. You will have to:

- read academic texts and make your own notes
- carry out your own research or experiments
- write essays, reports or a dissertation
- submit coursework and take exams.

What if you need help?

Signing up for a distance-learning course doesn't mean you'll be on your own. Most providers offer a variety of different ways for students to stay in touch with lecturers and tutors to get the support they need. For example, as well as traditional methods, such as phone and email, you may also be able to join online discussion forums, read blogs and attend study days to discuss your questions with academic staff.

Lots of distance-learning providers offer general help on organising your time, planning your work, essay writing and study skills. Getting help and advice in the early stages of your course can make it easier for you to get into the swing of distance learning.

If you want to contact other students on your course, most providers offer ways for you to do this. For example, some have their own Facebook pages for particular courses or subjects. Some of the larger providers also have student clubs and societies, which can help you meet new friends.

Who provides distance-learning degree courses?

Probably more organisations than you realise! You will certainly recognise some of the providers mentioned below, but others may be new to you. This list is not exhaustive and if you have a subject in mind it's certainly worth doing your own research.

Open University

The OU is the biggest university in the UK with over 250,000 students – it's also one of the most popular and regularly comes top of student satisfaction surveys (such as the National Student Survey). It offers more than 60 degree courses in areas such as arts and humanities, mathematics and statistics, science, education and engineering. Students can visit their local OU centre, where they can meet advisers, attend day schools or take part in social events. www.open.ac.uk.

Other universities

A number of universities in the UK offer distance-learning degree courses. For example, the University of London, www.londoninternational.ac.uk, and the University of Derby, www.derby.ac.uk/online, are two providers that offer a wide range of online courses.

BPP

BPP University College offers degrees in business studies and law, which can be studied entirely online. www.bpp.com.

International Correspondence Schools Ltd (ICS)

ICS offers a number of degree courses from UK universities including Anglia Ruskin University and the University of East London. www.icslearn.co.uk/distance-learning-degree.

RDI (Resource Development International)

RDI offers degree courses delivered by distance learning, in association with a number of UK universities. RDI also offers a number of HND courses by distance learning too, which, with further study, can be topped up to a degree. www.rdi.co.uk.

To search for distance learning degree courses, visit the Hotcourses website: www.hotcourses.com.

Things to bear in mind

Before you sign up for any course you should make sure you know the answers to these questions.

Does the course lead to a recognised degree? Unfortunately there are some fake organisations out there and it's important that you are certain the provider you are intending to register with is legitimate before you hand over any money. The following website, run by the Department for Business, Innovation & Skills, allows you to search for recognised bodies (who have the powers to award degrees) and listed bodies (who deliver courses that lead to degrees from recognised bodies). If the provider you

are considering is not listed on here, seek further independent advice before committing yourself.
www.bis.gov.uk/policies/higher-education/recognised-uk-degrees.

What do the fees cover? Some providers charge extra for assessments, study materials and study days. If this is true of the provider you're interested in, make sure you are clear about how much extra cost this is likely to add.

Does your course require any particular software? Your course provider will probably expect you to submit your assignments in a certain format, perhaps using a particular software program. Save yourself hassle later and check this out before you sign up.

Choosing the right job to support your studies

Whichever way you choose to study part time (with a college, university or through a distance-learning course) you'll also need to consider what type of work you want to do in your spare time. It may be that you already have a part-time job, but if you don't or if you're looking for a new job that could earn you more money, it's worth considering the following.

Could you find a job related to the subject that you're studying? You might think that because you're not qualified yet this isn't an option for you, but think again. Almost every organisation employs people in support roles, such as administrators and receptionists. Even if the job you get is not in the role or at the level you would eventually aim for, working for a relevant employer might just give you a foot in the door and the chance to network with relevant people. Working in a support role can also help you to get a feel for what the industry is about and current trends.

Will your paid work involve set days and hours? Will your course involve set days and hours? Are these likely to change depending on the term? If you know you will be available to work on particular days, you'll be able to look for a position during those times. However if you know your study times will vary it might be worth looking for employers that you know will be flexible.

Will your paid job allow you enough time to study? How many hours are you planning to work? How demanding is the job you have in mind? All degree courses involve a lot of self-directed study and you need to ensure that you'll have enough time and energy to do this.

Employer-funded study

Some employers incorporate HE qualifications into their training programmes. If you're keen to get a degree, are willing to work hard and would rather avoid the cost of tuition fees altogether, then employer-funded training may be the answer for you. This route to getting a degree combines on- and off-the-job training with a relevant job. However, unlike the part-time routes mentioned earlier, your studies would be tied in with your job. You would learn 'on-the-job' and spend the majority of your time working, but would have time off to study. Some employers for example, might expect you to work four days a week and spend one day at college or university. Your employer would be involved in your route to qualification; not only would they be financing your studies, they may also help you develop in your career by offering you the support and guidance you need to progress. You would also use your experiences at work to help you reflect on what you are learning for your qualification.

There are a couple of ways in which you could start training with an employer. You could:

- find a job with an employer that offers the chance to work towards a degree, or
- complete a Higher Apprenticeship.

A huge number of employers support their staff in gaining qualifications. However these opportunities are not always advertised. In many cases it may be the employee who approaches the employer to request training or the chance to work towards a qualification.

Exactly how you will study for your qualification will depend on your employer. However, it might involve:

- training in the workplace
- studying at a college or university for a day a week
- learning in your own time
- completing a distance-learning course.

Your training may involve more than one of these things.

Will you get a degree?

The exact qualification you will achieve will depend on the employer and what they are offering. Many employers offer the chance to work towards a foundation degree or HNC/D. As described in Chapter three, these qualifications relate to a particular area of work and are therefore particularly suitable for people who want to work and learn at the same time. You can 'top up' a foundation degree or HND to a full honours degree with further study, which your employer may well be interested in funding.

What are the advantages?

There are a lot of benefits to learning while you earn. Probably the biggest advantage is that your employer pays for your training – so you won't have to. You'll also be earning a salary. So there's no need to get into debt at all!

Depending on your employer, you may also get:

- paid time off to study
- support to complete your study and someone to talk to about your progress.

This route to a degree also means you will be getting valuable experience in your chosen field. It may take you a little longer than your peers to get a degree but by the time you graduate you'll have a few years of solid work experience on your CV, a job and an established relationship with your employer.

Employers that offer training

If this route sounds attractive to you, then you need to do your homework. You will need to have a career in mind, and one that's possible to qualify for through part-time study.

Employer-funded training isn't always easy to find, so you'll need to be thorough in your research and possibly look at employers you might not have considered before. Remember to look for employers that would be willing to fund further learning, even if they don't run any specific training schemes themselves.

Sector Skills Councils (SSCs) sometimes have information on employer schemes on their websites. Find out which SSC covers the career you are interested in and get in touch. Most of the Councils have advice teams or helplines, which can be a useful starting place. A directory of SSCs can be found on: www.sscalliance.org.

You could also **research employers in your local area**. Speak to the human resources departments of employers you are interested in and look at vacancies on their websites. Most will give some indication of how they are willing to support the development and training of their staff. Look at every option, even if you've never considered an organisation before.

You could also look at the **NotGoingToUni website**, which has vacancies especially suitable for people looking to work and learn. See: www.notgoingtouni.co.uk.

Below are just a few examples of employer-funded training schemes that could offer you the chance to gain a HE qualification. There may be others available in the sectors that are of interest to you. Individuals on these schemes are employed and receive a salary; their training (including courses fees) is funded by their employer. For further details on entry requirements for each of these schemes, see the websites listed.

- **Asda** has recently launched a new scheme for those interested in retail fashion. Successful applicants will be offered a salaried role at the headquarters of the company's fashion arm, George, and work towards a foundation degree in retail management. Those who complete the programme will also be offered the chance to top up their qualification to a BA Honours degree in retail. More information can be found on: www.george.jobs.

- **Tesco** offers existing employees the chance to work towards a foundation degree in retail. You would spend three days at university each term and also study online. More information on the vacancies available at Tesco is on: www.tesco-careers.com.

- **Barclays** (the banking group) runs a retail development programme. You would be based in a branch and work towards a BA Honours degree in management and leadership over three years. As well as learning on the job, you would attend Ashcroft International Business School (part of Anglia Ruskin University) for study blocks of two/four weeks. More information on the programme is available on: www.barclaysdegree.com.

- **Balfour Beatty Rail UK**, the UK's largest supplier of railway infrastructure, has a number of opportunities for trainee engineers interested in the rail industry. You would work towards either an HNC or HND in civil engineering or a foundation degree in rail engineering. You would attend college/university on a block- or day-realise basis. More details are on: www.bbrailjobs.com.

- **National Grid**, which operates the high-voltage electricity transmission network and high-pressure gas transmission system in Britain, runs an engineer training programme. There are a number of pathways within the programme including substations, power systems operations and electricity construction. You would receive on-the-job training and attend a specialist training centre where you would work towards a foundation degree in engineering. Further details are available on: www.nationalgridcareers.com.

The UCAS foundation degree website, http://fd.ucas.com, also lists a number of employers that offer their staff the opportunity to work towards a foundation degree. Some of these employers may only offer employees the chance to work towards HE qualifications as and when the business need arises.

Higher Apprenticeships

Higher Apprenticeships are a work-based learning route for people wishing to achieve HE qualifications. Training lasts for around three years and leads to a foundation degree, HNC/D, degree or professional qualification. In some areas, completion of a Higher Apprenticeship may be a starting point for registering for professional status.

The following Higher Apprenticeships lead to a foundation degree, HNC/D or honours degree:

- engineering technology
- contact centres
- ICT.

Remember that a foundation degree or HND can be topped up to an honours degree with further study.

These Higher Apprenticeships lead to professional qualifications at level 4:

- accounting
- purchasing and supply.

The following new frameworks are also being developed and should be available shortly:

- business and administration
- leadership and management

- construction
- food and drink
- life sciences
- health (proposed pathways include acute care support, maternity support and rehabilitation support).

Information about when these pathways will be available hasn't been released at the time of writing, but it's worth contacting the relevant SSC for more information. SSCs are a useful source of information on Higher Apprenticeships, and should be able to tell you if there are any available in the career area you are interested in.

Apprentices are employed and receive a salary. As an apprentice you will receive on-the-job training and attend a college, university or training centre to complete your academic work. You might go to college/ university one day a week, or for blocks of a few weeks. Apprenticeships are recognised by employers and offer a package of training that is built around the skills and competences you need to achieve to be able to do the job you are training for. As well as your HE or professional qualification, you will also work towards achieving:

- a competence-based qualification, such as an NVQ Diploma
- functional skills.

For more general information on Higher Apprenticeships, or to log on to the online vacancy matching service where you can search for Apprenticeship vacancies, see: www.apprenticeships.org.uk.

For more information on employer-sponsored study, see Chapter two.

Is part-time study right for you?

Although it can be a fantastic way of getting a qualification and avoiding massive debts, studying part time isn't for everyone, so you need to be honest with yourself before you apply for any courses. Studying after a day at work and at weekends takes motivation and commitment; will you be prepared to juggle the demands of a job with your course and study when your friends and family are relaxing? You should also bear in mind that if you're studying part time it obviously takes longer to complete a course – are you committed enough to keep it up for a few years?

All of this might sound a bit daunting, but there are thousands of people who manage to successfully juggle studying with the demands of a job, and there's no reason why, with the right commitment, you can't do it too! You'll have to work hard, but you'll be rewarded with a qualification and a better-looking bank balance.

Final thoughts

Studying on a part-time basis can help you avoid some of the debt associated with gaining a degree through the traditional full-time route. Going part time may not be a route that you've thought of before, but it isn't just for mature students. This chapter has explored the ways in which you could study part time and hopefully highlighted options that could work for you. Perhaps the most important thing to take away from this chapter is a realisation that you do have options. Find out what's available in the area you're interested in and look into employer-funded study – there may well be more opportunities than you think.

Ask yourself...

- Could a part-time degree course work for you?

- Would you enjoy working while you're studying?

- Are there part-time courses that are suitable for you?

- What training opportunities could relevant employers offer you?

- Could you handle the demands of working and studying at the same time?

Chapter five

Location UK

Your two biggest costs when you go to university will be your tuition fees and living expenses. Both of these can vary widely depending on where you choose to live and study, so it makes sense to do your research and look for the most cost-effective options for you. This chapter will cover:

- tuition fees in England, Wales, Northern Ireland and Scotland
- accommodation costs
- the financial benefits of living at home
- other living costs including food, insurance and travel.

Tuition fees in the UK

How much you will have to pay (if anything) in course tuition fees will vary depending on:

- whether you come from England, Wales, Northern Ireland or Scotland
- how much is charged by the university for your chosen course.

Where there are tuition fees, not all universities will charge the maximum they are allowed to charge. You may find that even within the same university, course fees will vary. Although you shouldn't decide to take a course just because the fees are low, you don't want to be saddled with unnecessary debt. Because university tuition fees are rising, it makes sense to shop around for a course that's good value for money. As described in Chapter one, you need to think like an investor.

If you do have to pay tuition fees, you don't have to pay them up-front – you can normally take out a low-interest loan for all or part of your fees and you don't have to start paying this back until you're in a job and earning a certain salary – this has been set at £21,000 for students from England who start university in 2012.

Tuition fees can change from year to year, so make sure that you get the most up-to-date information. Unless otherwise stated, the figures in the following table are based on students starting university for the first time in the academic year 2012/13. At the time of writing, funding plans for Wales, Northern Ireland and Scotland are to be confirmed. For up to date information, see: www.ucas.com/students/studentfinance.

Maximum tuition fees based on where you come from and where you study

	Study in England	Study in Wales	Study in Northern Ireland	Study in Scotland**
From England	Up to £9,000 a year	Up to £9,000 a year	To be confirmed	To be confirmed (fees for 2011/12 £1,820 or £2,895 for medicine)
From Wales	Up to £3,375* (plus any small inflationary rise)	Up to £3,375* (plus any small inflationary rise)	Up to £3,375* (plus any small inflationary rise)	Up to £3,375* (plus any small inflationary rise)
From Northern Ireland	Up to £9,000 a year	Up to £9,000 a year	To be confirmed	To be confirmed (fees for 2011/12 £1,820 or £2,895 for medicine)
From Scotland (N.B. Scottish degree courses are normally four years)	Up to £9,000 a year	Up to £9,000 a year	To be confirmed	To be confirmed (no fees for 2011/12); students may have to pay a graduate contribution

*If you're from Wales, regardless of where in the UK you want to study, you won't be charged more than £3,375 because the Welsh Assembly Government proposes providing a fee waiver grant to cover any difference between the amount charged by your university and the amount you have to pay. This is yet to be confirmed.

**Financial arrangements for students from Scotland have always been very different from the rest of the UK. In fact, Scottish students have not had to pay tuition fees at all in the last few years.

Remember that some universities will charge less than the maximum fees quoted in the table.

As you can see from the figures in the table, where you decide to study can have a big impact on how much you'll have to pay in tuition fees. While, at present, studying in Scotland looks tempting financially, consider the additional travel costs, the fact that courses normally last for four years and whether the courses on offer would suit you. Make sure you get all the information you need.

Financial support

Apart from checking out course fees and loans, it's worth finding out whether you're entitled to any financial support or fee waiver based on where you study. For instance, regardless of where you are from in the UK, if your household income is less than around £18,000 and you study at a Welsh university, you may be entitled to a Welsh National Bursary.

Other bursaries and awards are based on your household income, background or other factors, so find out what you are entitled to and make sure you claim everything you can!

Find out more

Chapter eight has some information on the financial support you may be entitled to. You can get information by contacting the relevant finance organisation. If you're from:

- England – tel: 0845 300 50 90, or see:
  www.direct.gov.uk/studentfinance

- Wales – tel: 0845 602 8845, or view:
  www.studentfinancewales.co.uk

- Northern Ireland – tel: 0845 600 0662, or see:
  www.studentfinanceni.co.uk

- Scotland – tel: 0300 555 05 05, or look at: www.saas.gov.uk

Accommodation costs

Unless you're a very big spender, you'll find that your major cost while you're a student is rent. How much you'll have to pay usually reflects the cost of living in different areas of the UK. Living in London and the south-east is usually more expensive than most other regions. Apart from where you study, how much you pay for rent also depends on the kind of accommodation you go for.

The main accommodation options are described below. Find out what kind of accommodation is available for each university you are considering and get an idea of costs.

Living in university halls of residence

Many universities provide halls of residence or other university-owned accommodation. Halls are popular with first-year students because they're a good place to settle into university life and to meet other freshers. Often students 'live out' during the second and third years of their course. Find out the rules for allocating rooms – are you guaranteed a place, at least in the first year?

Halls are either:

- catered – where some or all of your meals are provided and included in the cost of your accommodation

or

- self-catered – where there are equipped kitchens so that you can cook for yourself, or a group of you can take it in turns to cook for each other. Alternatively you could eat at canteens or restaurants on or off the campus and have takeaways. However, if you did this on a regular basis, the costs would soon add up!

Obviously you'll pay more if meals are included, but it could still work out cheaper than cooking for yourself. Catered halls might appeal to you if you're no Jamie Oliver or if your time to shop and cook is limited.

Initially you may think that the costs are high, but you could end up paying less for halls of residence than for private accommodation because the fees usually include things like utility bills, internet access and insurance. Another benefit of living in halls is that they are normally near the university or on campus, so this would cut your travel costs and time.

If you go on the UCAS website, www.ucas.com, you'll find a map and an alphabetical list of universities throughout the UK. You can click on any university you are interested in to find an estimate of weekly costs for accommodation managed by the institution, i.e. university-owned halls of residence and other types of properties. Prices vary, for example at the University of London, you could pay up to £140 a week for accommodation with meals, whereas at the University of Sunderland, you could pay as little as £55 without food.

Renting privately

Your other main option is to rent privately – this could be a:

- flat or studio apartment
- house (usually shared with others)
- room in a private hall of residence
- room in someone's home.

Sometimes universities rent properties from private landlords and then sublet them to students. This can guarantee a certain standard of accommodation and a fair rent. You can also rent directly from a private landlord.

If you live on your own, it's likely to cost more than if you share a property with other students. Another option would be to rent a room in a house and live with the owner, perhaps a family. If you'll be living with other people, make sure that you are likely to get along. Agree in advance who will pay for what, how meals will be cooked and what's acceptable behaviour. In other words, work out some ground rules from the start!

The cost of private accommodation will vary depending on a number of factors including the property's location, size and condition, and how close it is to the university or to good transport links.

To get an idea of rental costs in areas where you are interested in studying, go online. For example, www.accommodationforstudents.com allows you to search for student houses, flats and private halls in university towns and cities across the UK; you can use this to compare typical rents. Also, most universities have a student accommodation office – staff there can give you an idea of how much you will have to pay and can help you find suitable accommodation.

To give you an idea of costs, a 2010 survey by Accommodation for Students found that:

- the average weekly rent for students across Britain was around £65 (although other surveys put the figure nearer £99)

- the highest student rents were in London, with private student accommodation costing an average of £103 a week

- average rents were also expensive – at least £80 a week – in Brighton, Cambridge, Egham, Exeter, Guildford, Kingston, Middlesex, St Andrews and Uxbridge

- average weekly student rents in some other major university cities included Birmingham at £57, Liverpool £55, Manchester £60 and Sheffield £60

- the cheapest rents were in Middlesbrough at £42 a week, while weekly student rents were also low at £50 a week or less in Crewe, Hull, Pontypridd, Stockton and Stoke-on-Trent.

Homeshare

Although it might not be everyone's cup of tea, you could consider a homeshare programme. This is where you are matched to live with a vulnerable older person (known as the householder). Instead of paying the going rent or any rent at all, you agree to provide help and support to the householder and will probably contribute towards bills.

A homeshare can be a valuable life experience and you could mention it when applying for further courses, training or jobs in the future. It's particularly relevant experience if you're looking to work in a caring role.

There are a number of schemes operating around the country – including in Oxford, London and Bristol. If the idea appeals to you, find out more at: www.naaps.org.uk/en/homeshare.

Questions to ask about rent or hall fees

Because not everything is always as it seems, make sure you find out as much as possible about your rent or hall fees. Ask lots of questions.

- How much is the rent or fee?

- Is it payable each week, month or term?

- What does the rent or fee include? For instance, will it cover utility bills (water, heating etc), the TV licence, cleaning and broadband connection?

- If meals are included, on what basis?

- Does the rent have to be paid during university vacations?

- How much is the deposit? What are the terms?

- Do you have to clear out your belongings during vacations? If so, you may have to pay storage costs or arrange for your things to be taken home.

Before you sign anything, make sure you read your rental contract or tenancy agreement carefully. It's always worth asking whether there's room for any negotiation on the rent.

Living with the folks

Staying at home whilst taking a degree course can work out a lot cheaper than living away. So, if there's a suitable course at a university or further education college near you, it's certainly worth considering.

Don't worry that you'll be alone. Increasing numbers of students under the age of 21 – an estimated 35%, in fact – are opting to apply to universities within 25 miles of where they live. This means there are likely to be other students in your situation so you won't necessarily be missing out on student life.

Money matters

If you decide to live at home and you're one of the very lucky ones, your family won't expect you to pay for a thing! The reality is that most students aren't able to freeload. You'll probably be expected to make a contribution to your 'board and lodging'. Even so, because hall fees and private rents are such a major cost, you should still make some savings.

Before you decide to live at home, it's a good idea to get the answers to some key questions, such as those listed below.

- How much will your family charge you?

- Will they want paying weekly, monthly or each term?

- What's included in your payment, e.g. will it cover food, TV licence, utility bills and laundry?

- Will you have to pay anything during university vacations?

- How much will it cost to get to and from the university for lectures, tutorials, socialising etc?

Bear in mind that, although you may save money in rent and other expenses if you live at home, you may not be entitled to as big a student loan for living costs. For example, in the year 2011/12, students from England could apply for an income-assessed Maintenance Loan each year of up to £4,950 or £6,928 in London, but only £3,838 if living at home.

Another advantage of living at home is that if you already have a part-time job, you may be able to continue with this when you start your degree course. Even if you don't have paid work, you may find it easier to find a job because you'll be familiar with the area and the kind of opportunities available; you may even have ready-made contacts.

The reality of living at home

Apart from saving money on rent and other living costs, there are other advantages to living at home. These include:

- less general upheaval
- possibly more peace and quiet to get on with your studies
- the ability to keep up with friends from school and the local area
- easier to retain existing interests, hobbies or other commitments.

If you do decide to live at home, it may be hard for your parents to accept that you're an adult; at the same time, you'll probably want to have a good university experience and more freedom than you may have had in the past. To prevent problems in the future, it's a good idea to sit down with your family to establish some ground rules so that everyone respects each other. Talk about things like cooking and cleaning arrangements and what's acceptable in terms of bringing friends home, coming home late at night and so on.

Other living costs

Apart from rent, your other living costs will vary depending on where you live and study.

Food, clothes, household goods, personal items etc

You often have to pay more for food, bits and pieces for your home, toiletries and other items in more expensive or remote areas of the country. This may be because you have less choice of supermarkets and other stores in some places.

Insurance

Insurance for your personal belongings, and your car or motorbike if you have one, will normally be more expensive in more disadvantaged areas as the risk of crime is considered greater, so this is something to think about. Check costs with insurance companies, such as Endsleigh, who specialise in student insurance.

The daily commute

Another factor to think about is the cost of daily travel to university sites and to areas where you want to socialise. Although rents further away from the university can work out cheaper, remember that additional travel costs can add up, especially if you are late going home and have to pay for taxis after the buses or trains have stopped running.

It's great if you can safely walk or cycle. If this isn't possible, find out the cost of public transport – buses, trams, tubes or trains. Rather than paying daily, find out whether you can buy a cheaper weekly or monthly travel pass and whether there are any student discounts. For instance, if you live in London, you can apply for an 18+ Student Oyster photocard. This will save you 30% on adult travelcards and bus and tram passes; find out more at: www.tfl.gov.uk.

If you need to have a car or motorbike, work out how much this will cost to run. Also get an idea of where you can park and parking charges.

Travelling home

You may be a home bird and want to travel back to see your family on a regular basis. If so, find out the best way of doing this and work out the costs involved. If you come from Cornwall and want to study in Aberdeen, for example, the cost and time taken to travel may make it difficult for you to visit your family during term time. This is a factor to consider when choosing where to study.

Although a car or motorbike may give you more freedom to travel home when you want, think about whether you really need one. Work out how much a vehicle will cost to run; factor in tax, insurance, fuel, parking and other expenses. Public transport may be a cheaper option.

Find out about various student travel cards. For example:

- the **16-25 Railcard** gives you a third off train fares; it costs £26 for one year or £65 for three; for more information, see: www.16-25railcard.co.uk

- the **Young Persons Coachcard** gives full-time students up to 30% off National Express fares. The card costs £10 for one year, or £25 for three; find out more on: www.nationalexpress.com/coach/offers.

Work-life balance – your leisure time

Socialising

It's important to relax from time to time and, along with most other students, you'll probably want to spend some time hanging out with your friends. You may enjoy a few pints in the pub, dancing in clubs, going to gigs, eating out or seeing the latest cinema release. Although some cities, such as London, are renowned for being more expensive than others, how much you spend will also depend on where you like to go and what you like to do.

Most large university towns and cities have a wide range of venues and there are sometimes discounts for students. Socialising at the student union can work out cheaper than going out on the town.

Try to get an idea of how much it'll cost for a typical night out at any university town or city you are considering. Factor in:

- entry or ticket prices
- the cost of drinks – a recent survey found that a pint of beer can vary from as little as £1.35 at the University of Liverpool to £2.54 at the University of Brighton
- any travel costs – especially if you need to take a taxi.

Other interests

If you enjoy a particular activity, hobby or interest, find out whether the universities you are interested in have any clubs or associations you could join. Most have a huge range of societies – ranging from American football to yoga – and joining one of these can be cheaper than trying to find a similar group elsewhere. Membership fees are likely to be kept to a minimum and you probably won't have so far to travel.

Laundry

As mundane as it may sound, if you live away from home, you'll probably need to wash some clothes, towels and bed linen from time to time. Find out whether there are facilities on campus as these might be cheaper than using high street laundrettes. In most university halls of residence there's a laundry room and bed linen changes may be included in your hall fees.

Final thoughts

Where you end up studying really can make a big difference to how much you'll have to fork out for your university education. When you compare different courses, try to estimate how these various costs will impact on you. This chapter will have given you much food for thought.

Ask yourself...

- How much do different universities charge for the course you want to do?

- What kind of university experience do you want? For example, do you want to live on campus in halls? Are you keen to go to a big city like London or Edinburgh or would a smaller town suit you?

- What are the cheapest accommodation options where you want to study?

- Would you be prepared to share accommodation with people you don't know?

- Would you get fully involved in student life if you opt to live at home?

- In what other ways could you minimise your living costs?

Chapter six

Broaden your horizons

The option to study abroad has never been more attractive. With big hikes in tuition fees in the UK, you could make great savings. In fact, both tuition fees and living expenses can work out cheaper in other countries, so even if it isn't something you ever imagined doing, it's worth thinking about studying overseas. This chapter will cover:

- the reasons why you should consider studying abroad

- taking part of your course abroad

- taking your entire course overseas – in Europe or beyond

- money matters – tuition fees and other study costs, and the scholarships, grants and other awards you could receive

- research, planning and other things you need to consider, such as speaking the language and degree recognition.

To study overseas, you don't have to take languages or a course with a European or international dimension. You can choose to study any subject – from archaeology to zoology.

More students are spreading their wings

The world can be your oyster! Traditionally it's not been the done thing for students from the UK to venture overseas to study. In fact, according to statistics from the Academic Cooperation Association, just one student from the UK goes overseas to study for every 20 who come to the UK. But things are changing rapidly. Over the past few years, there's been a big increase in the number of students opting to go to university abroad.

- A study by the Department for Business, Innovation and Skills in 2011 found that a record 22,000 UK students were on full-time higher education programmes overseas.

- Record numbers of students from the UK – around 12,000 – are now studying in another European country through the Erasmus programme (see later in this chapter).

- More British students than ever before are heading Stateside to study. Over 4,000 undergraduate students from the UK are currently studying in the USA.

Why study abroad?

If you study at a university overseas, apart from saving money in the short term, as explained in Chapter one, the very experience can add value to your investment in higher education. There are lots of reasons why you should think about studying overseas – just some are listed below.

- Tuition fees are often lower than in the UK; sometimes there are no fees at all! Even where tuition fees are charged, you may be able to get a scholarship or some other financial support based on your academic abilities or financial need.

- The cost of living can work out cheaper in other areas of the world.

- As it's becoming harder to get into universities in the UK, looking further afield may give you a better chance of getting on a course.

- Studying abroad will allow you to experience a different education system and perhaps enable you to approach your subject from a new perspective.

- The opportunity will take you out of your comfort zone, so it can help make you more confident and independent.

- It will give you the chance to develop your interpersonal skills. It'll show that you are flexible, willing to adapt to new situations and prepared to take on a challenge.

- You may have the chance to learn another language. In non-English speaking countries, even if you're taught in English, you're bound to pick up some of the local language.

- In a competitive job market, spending time studying abroad will give you that bit extra on your CV. It'll give you something to talk about in interviews, make you stand out from the crowd and could help you land your dream job!

- It could boost your employment prospects, particularly if you want to work overseas, for a multinational company or for a firm that does business abroad.

- A period studying abroad is likely to give you an amazing life experience. You'll meet all kinds of people from different backgrounds and cultures!

Taking part of your course abroad

Rather than opting to take your whole degree overseas, you could take part of it at a university abroad. This might be through Erasmus (see below) or another scheme.

Although there are lots of higher education courses that include a year abroad - either for study or work experience - these usually add a year to your course, so would not necessarily save you money in the same way as the initiatives described below.

Erasmus

Erasmus is the European Commission's flagship educational exchange programme:

- through the programme, you can spend from three months to a full academic year studying in another European Union (EU) country as part of your higher education course

- over 4,000 universities in 31 countries across Europe participate in the programme

- you don't have to be studying languages - the scheme is for students of any subject

- you may need a good working knowledge of the language of the country where you intend to study, but not all courses require you to be fluent. Some universities offer courses in English and others provide language tuition. There's more information on learning the language later in this chapter.

Saving money through Erasmus

- If you spend a full academic year on an Erasmus programme, you don't have to pay any tuition fees for that year, either to your home or EU university.

- If you spend less than a year on the programme, you normally just have to pay a proportion of your UK tuition fees.

- You will continue to receive any student grant or loan to which you are entitled from UK sources.

- You will also be given an Erasmus grant. This contributes to the extra costs you may have to pay for studying abroad, such as flights home. A win-win situation!

For more information, contact the British Council Erasmus Unit on: 029 2092 4311, or see: www.britishcouncil.org/erasmus.

University partnerships and links abroad

Many UK universities or particular university departments or courses, have links or partnerships with universities abroad. If you spend some time studying abroad at a partner institution, you may be awarded a stand-alone qualification for your period of study abroad or your achievements might contribute towards your overall degree. If you are interested in this option, find out more about tuition fees and living costs. You can get information from your international or study abroad office at your chosen university in the UK.

Studying at a UK university campus overseas

More and more UK universities are setting up campuses overseas. Here they offer their own degree courses to international students who want a British higher education but who can't afford or don't want to come to the UK to study.

If your university has a campus abroad, you may have the option to take part of your degree there. Middlesex University, for example, allows you to combine study in London with a year or more of the equivalent degree in Dubai and/or Mauritius; during your time overseas, you pay local tuition fees. The cost of living and accommodation can work out a lot cheaper in some countries where there are UK university campuses.

Taking your entire course abroad

If you want to take your whole degree overseas, you could consider:

- studying in another European country

- going further afield, for example to another Commonwealth country or to the USA

- taking a degree at a UK university abroad.

Staying in Europe

Under EU rules, all students from EU member states who attend universities in the EU must be treated the same as local applicants with regard to fees. This means you cannot be charged more for tuition fees than a national of that country would be charged. Fees are usually much lower in other EU countries than in the UK and some universities charge no fees at all.

You are entitled to the same grants to cover tuition fees as those available to a national of that country. However, you may not have the same entitlement to grants and loans for living costs. This doesn't mean that this type of financial support isn't available, but you will need to check what support you can claim.

To be entitled to EU tuition rates etc, there may be certain EU residency requirements. If you haven't been living in the UK for long, you should find out what the criteria are.

Venturing outside Europe

The USA

When Americans say that they are at 'college' what they usually mean is that they are taking a university degree. There are both private and public universities in the States; public universities receive some state funding so their tuition fees are often cheaper. Fees generally are pretty high at US universities but, as described later in this chapter, scholarships maybe available and you may find the cost of living lower in some areas.

If you're keen on the idea of studying in the States, the US-UK Fulbright Commission is the official source of advice. The Fulbright website, www.fulbright.co.uk, has all kinds of information on courses, applications and funding. Every year, Fulbright hosts a USA College Day fair in London. This would give you an opportunity to ask representatives from US universities for specific information about admission exams, fees, how you go about applying to their institutions etc. Fulbright also runs a series of evening seminars for students and their parents.

Commonwealth countries

Many people in the UK have strong ties with family and friends in other Commonwealth countries. If this is the case, staying with them while you study could save you lots of money in accommodation costs. Just having contacts in a country may give you the confidence you need to move overseas to study, as some local support would be there should you need it. Even if you don't stay with family or friends, you may find that the cost of living is cheaper in some Commonwealth countries.

If you're thinking of applying to a university in another Commonwealth country – such as Australia, Canada, India, Jamaica, New Zealand, Nigeria, Pakistan or South Africa – The Association of Commonwealth Universities can give you advice; see the website for information and a course search facility: www.acu.ac.uk.

Other countries

Although English-speaking countries, such as the USA and many Commonwealth nations, may be the first places you might consider, remember that there are many other areas of the world where you could study – Africa, Asia, South America or non-EU countries in Eastern Europe, for instance – where both tuition fees and living costs may be a lot lower. If you're interested in finding out more, contact the relevant embassy, consulate or education office.

Studying at a UK university campus abroad

As mentioned earlier in this chapter, UK universities are increasingly setting up campuses overseas. As a UK student, you could opt to take your whole degree at a British university with a campus abroad – you'd get exactly the same degree as you would in the UK. Tuition fees will vary but may be less than at home. In addition, living and accommodation costs are often a lot lower than in the UK. Find out more from your chosen university.

Money, money, money

If you decide to study overseas, at the present time it's unlikely that you'll be entitled to any funding sources that would be available for you to study in the UK. However, the UK is committed to the principle of the portability of educational loans and grants, so in the future this may be possible.

If you decide to study overseas rather than in the UK, be aware that you'll probably have to:

- pay your tuition fees and living costs yourself without the help of low-interest government loans

- pay your fees up front.

As mentioned earlier in this chapter, if you are a UK citizen and study in another EU member country, you don't have to pay any more than local tuition fees at your chosen university.

If you don't have enough savings, perhaps you could work for a while to help fund your studies or there may be other ways of raising the money. If you're lucky, your family may be prepared to help you out. If you can persuade a lender to give you the money, another option is to take out a loan. However, unlike government loans for tuition fees and living costs available to students studying in the UK, normal interest rates will apply and you would probably have to start making payments immediately. If you study in Europe and do a vocational course, you could be entitled to take out a Professional and Career Development Loan – for information, see: www.direct.gov.uk/pcdl.

You may have to show in advance that you have the means to pay your overseas tuition fees, either from your own resources or from a pre-approved loan. It may also be a condition of admission that you can show you would be able to support yourself throughout the course.

Tuition fees

Fees for courses vary greatly around the world, but even before planned rises from 2012, university fees in England, Wales and Northern Ireland are already higher than the majority of other countries.

It would be impossible to list all the fees charged by universities around the world. However, to give you an idea of what you might be expected to pay, the table below gives just a few examples of the tuition fees being charged (or not, as the case might be) to UK students in different countries.

Remember that policies on fees change from year to year, so make sure you are armed with the most recent information. The figures in the table are only approximate and you should check up-to-date exchange rates.

Comparison of fees in different countries

Country	Typical fees charged to students from the UK	Approximate equivalent cost per year in £s
Australia	$10,000 to $20,000 a year (Australian $)	£6,300 to £12,600
China	From around 13,000 RMB a year (Chinese Yuan)	From £1,250
France	Depending on the course, from around €200 a year	From £175
Germany	No fees at many universities; under €500 per semester at others (there are two semesters a year)	£860 or under, where fees charged
Spain	From around €10 per credit (there are normally 240 credits in a degree – around 60 a year for a four year course)	From £540 (based on around £9 a credit)
The Netherlands	Around €1,700 a year	Around £1,500
USA	Fees vary widely – the average is around $32,000 per year at private universities and $24,500 at public universities	£20,000 average at private universities; £15,000 average at public universities
Austria, Denmark, Ireland, Sweden	Among the countries where fees are not currently charged	£0
UK	*Depending on where you study, up to £9,000 a year from 2012*	*Up to £9,000 from 2012*

Scholarships, grants and other awards

Although scholarships are sometimes available, they are limited in supply, so competition is fierce.

Find out whether the university you are considering provides scholarships or other types of funding. For information on government-funded scholarships, contact the embassy, consulate or education office of the country where you want to go.

Make sure you apply for scholarships well in advance – normally a year or so before you intend to start your course.

Because the cost of studying in the **USA** is relatively expensive, around a third of British undergraduate students are on some kind of scholarship. Scholarships are based on merit and/or financial need; there are also some sports scholarships. To find out more, contact the US-UK Fulbright Commission on: 090 1488 0162 (Mondays and Thursdays from 1.30pm to 5.00pm), or see: www.fulbright.co.uk.

A limited number of scholarships are provided through the **Commonwealth Scholarships and Fellowships Plan** to help students study in certain other Commonwealth countries. Information can be found on: www.csfp-online.org.

A few UK-based educational trusts and charities may be prepared to support you, but any grants would only be small.

Living expenses

The cost of accommodation, food and other items vary from country to country and from city to city. What you pay out if you live and study in China might be minimal compared with the Scandinavian countries, for example.

Work out how much it'll cost you to live in the town or city where you want to study. Find out what kind of accommodation is available and how much this will cost. How does the cost of food and other items compare with where you live in the UK? Bear in mind that changes in currency exchange rates can have quite an impact and make actual costs unpredictable.

Additional costs

Apart from working out how much you'll have to pay in tuition fees and living costs, find out if there will be any extra expenses. For instance, consider the cost of:

- a longer course – many degree programmes overseas last for four years instead of the usual three at most universities in England, Wales and Northern Ireland

- any application, enrolment, student services or exam charges – these hidden extras can add up

- flights or other transport back to the UK for vacations and to visit your family and friends at home during term time if you need to

- any necessary language or other entry tests

- visas or permits – you can find out whether these are needed and how much they cost from the country's consulate, embassy or high commission

- health and other insurance
- any medical examinations you may have to undertake.

Paid work

Many students in the UK have a part-time job to help fund their studies. This isn't always possible in other countries.

- If you are on a student visa, check whether (and to what extent) you are able to work in the country of your choice.
- Find out whether course tutors actually mind you working – they may disapprove if there's a possibility it'll distract you from your studies; timetables can be very full on some courses.
- Check the availability of work too – jobs may be hard to come by.

Don't forget that you can always try to get paid work back in the UK during your university vacations, but being away from home may make it a bit harder to search for opportunities.

Research and planning

It makes sense to do as much research as possible as a whole new world of opportunities is open to you ... literally! This means much more choice and a potentially harder decision to make.

The more research and planning you do, the more likely you are to know what to expect and the quicker you'll be able to settle into university life. It'll also reduce the risk of making a false start and incurring unnecessary expenses.

Start planning as far in advance as possible. Give yourself up to 18 months to:

- do your research – find the answers to the questions listed below
- complete the application – you usually need to apply directly to the university or universities of interest to you; the UK is relatively unusual in having a centralised application system, UCAS
- take any necessary tests or exams
- obtain funding
- sort out visas or permits.

Questions to ask

The following questions may help you to work out whether studying abroad is right for you and, if so, how you can get good value for money from your degree. Although choosing the wrong country, university or course wouldn't be the end of the world, it could cost you more money than if you made the wrong choice in the UK.

Which country would suit you? Perhaps you've already been to a particular country and like the feel of the place. Or, you might have family or friends in a certain town or city overseas who would be able to provide you with support and even cheap or free accommodation.

What entry qualifications do you need? For entry to certain universities or courses, you may have to take a test or exam. Find out how acceptable your level 3 qualifications will be for entry to the course of your choice. Entry requirements are either set by the state or by individual universities.

What's the course like? Find out how demanding it is compared with similar courses in the UK. What topics are covered? How much scope is there to pick options, particularly later in the course? Are there any student satisfaction surveys you can access? If not, try getting an idea of drop-out rates and the destinations of previous students.

How's the course taught? How many hours of timetabled lectures and tutorials are there? How much private study is expected? What methods of teaching are used? In British universities there tends to be a lot of emphasis on independent study whereas in some other countries, study is more directed.

What are the facilities like for learning? Depending on your course, this could include laboratories, studios or libraries.

How many students are usually on the course? Class sizes may be much bigger than you would expect in the UK.

What kind of student support services are there? There may be less support and pastoral care than you would expect in the UK. Do students have access to a personal tutor or student mentor? If so, how much contact would you have with them?

What kind of social and leisure opportunities are there? In the UK there's a big tradition of universities having clubs and societies. This may or may not be the case at universities abroad. Much could depend on whether most students live at home or not. Find out how many students live on campus and whether they tend to go home at weekends.

What student accommodation is available? Some universities provide more accommodation than others, particularly for first-year students. If not, you may have to sort out your own place to stay.

How well does the university treat overseas students? The British Council's 2011 Global Gauge survey rated universities around the world according to how friendly they are towards overseas students. It used measures such as course quality, degree recognition and support for overseas students. The following were the top ten results:

Overseas student-friendly countries

1st	Germany
2nd	Australia
3rd	UK
4th	China
5th	Malaysia
6th	USA
7th	Japan
8th	Russia
9th	Nigeria
10th	Brazil

Ideally you should visit your chosen university in advance of applying. Doing this would help you to find the answers to lots of these questions. If this is impossible, try to make personal contacts; you could speak with course tutors or current students. Have a good look at university websites and prospectuses.

Speaking the lingo

English is widely spoken in many countries around the world – either as a first or second language. Even in non-English speaking countries, in order to attract more international students, a growing number of courses are being taught in English. It's still useful to have conversational ability in the country's main language so that you can get the most out of socialising with other students and living there.

If your course isn't going to be taught in English, ask yourself whether your language skills will be sufficient. Even if you speak the language, you may need to learn technical or academic terms to cope with your studies.

Be aware that, if your studies are not in English, you may have to take a language test. You are likely to have to pay a fee for this.

It's a good idea to take a language course before you start your degree course, perhaps in the UK before you leave. If you get the chance, however, it would be even better to go on a language course for overseas students at your chosen university before you start your degree programme. Apart from learning the language, this would give you a chance to understand a bit more about the culture, experience the education system, get to know the area and mix with other students. Whether in the UK or abroad, find out how much a language course will cost.

Recognition of qualifications

It's no good doing a degree if it isn't recognised in the UK or any other country where you might want to work or study in the future.

Investigate the reputation of the university and courses you are considering. Every year, various tables are produced showing how universities across the world rate against each other; for instance, you could use the:

- QS World University Rankings – these can be found at www.topuniversities.com – the website also gives information on universities worldwide and an idea of living costs in different countries

- *THE* World University Rankings – can be viewed at: www.timeshighereducation.co.uk/world-university-rankings.

Contact UK NARIC, or the equivalent organisation in any other country in which you intend to work or do further study, to find out how the degree you will get compares with those in the UK or elsewhere. UK NARIC is the national agency that provides information and advice on qualifications from over 180 countries. It's the only official source of information on international qualifications to individuals who wish to work or study in the UK. More information can be found through: www.naric.org.uk or www.enic-naric.net.

If you study in Europe, many higher education qualifications are recognised by other European countries, so you should be able to take up further study or a professional job anywhere in the EU. If you have a particular career in mind, the professional body for the occupation for which you hope to qualify should be able to give you advice. Information on the recognition of qualifications in Europe can be found on: www.europeopen.org.uk.

The European Credit Transfer System has helped with the academic recognition of higher education studies in Europe. The System allows you to study a unit of a course in another EU country and have it accredited towards your degree, as long as that unit is agreed to be equivalent to the one it replaces on your 'home' course.

Find out more

For information on the opportunities available, tuition fees, sources of funding, advice on study visas and so on, it's a good idea to start by contacting the embassy or high commission of the country where you are thinking of studying. Information is often also available on their websites. To search for the contact details and websites of foreign embassies in the UK, visit: www.fco.gov.uk.

The UK Council for International Student Affairs (UK CISA) can provide information to UK students who want to study abroad; call their advice line on 020 7107 9922 or see: www.ukcisa.org.uk.

If you want to study in another EU country, the 'Education & Youth' section of the European Commission website has useful information on access, fees, financial help and the recognition of qualifications: http://europa.eu/youreurope/citizens/education.

There are organisations and websites, e.g. www.studyabroaddirectory.com, that can help you find all kinds of information on universities overseas. In order to attract international students, most countries have organisations that help promote their own universities. For example, for information on studying in Australia or New Zealand, you can contact Study Options on: 020 7353 7200 or see: www.studyoptions.com. For information about studying in Canada, see: www.studyincanada.com.

EXODUS is a database of information about living, working and studying abroad – produced by Careers Europe, you may find this available in school, college or careers libraries.

Final thoughts

Studying overseas has the potential to save you a lot of money, but you do need to do your sums. If the option appeals to you, as recommended earlier in this chapter, start your research as soon as possible. This will give you time to check out tuition fees, living and other costs and to apply for scholarships and visas. Although you should try to talk to as many people as possible about your plans, do get impartial advice and make your own decisions.

Ask yourself...

- Have you got the confidence to go overseas to study?

- Have you thought about where in the world you'd like to go?

- How much are the tuition fees and other study costs for courses you'd like to do?

- Have you explored all the possible sources of funding?

- How does the cost of living compare with where you live in the UK?

- Will your degree be recognised by employers in the future?

Chapter seven

Maximise your income, minimise your debt

One way to help minimise the amount of money you will need to borrow while you're at university is to earn money either before your course (if you take a gap year) or while you study. This chapter will explore all the different ways you can earn money, from paid placements to part-time work in the student union bar! This chapter will look at:

- taking a gap year and ideas for gap-year jobs

- the value of earning while you're studying

- ideas for part-time jobs, including jobs on campus, jobs with perks and jobs that use your skills

- working during university vacations

- how to find a suitable job.

Taking a gap year

If you're keen to do a full-time, three-year degree course, one of the simplest things you could do to lessen the potential debt is to take a year out to earn money before you start.

In 2010, 6.9% of higher education applicants (over 34,000 students) accepted a place at university but deferred their entry until 2011. It is estimated that every year thousands of school leavers take a gap year. Many of these people go on to apply for university later.

The rise in tuition fees does mean it's likely that more young people will be planning to take a gap year in order to work and earn money for their studies. Getting work experience during your gap year takes planning and motivation, but it offers significant benefits other than just financial rewards. The most beneficial option is to find work experience that is relevant to your course and future career ambition, although any work undertaken can still prove useful. Besides earning some money, working for a year before your degree allows you to:

- gain practical, hands-on experience
- get an insight into the range of jobs available to you – what they involve and their potential progression routes
- 'try out' an employer to see if you like them
- start building a network of contacts
- develop an understanding of the 'world of work', which will eventually help you to settle into a permanent role more easily
- potentially gain a future referee, to use when applying for jobs after your degree.

Don't forget – working during your gap year also lets an employer 'try you out' to see if they like you! If you are successful, you might be able to secure yourself some work during the vacations or possibly get sponsorship for your degree. Your employer may even be able to offer you work after you graduate.

Ideas for gap-year jobs

If you're planning to keep your student debt as low as possible by taking a gap year to earn money, then you'll need to find a job quickly (once you've finished your level 3 studies) and look out for opportunities that pay enough to make it worth your while. To earn as much as possible you will want to find full-time work, in a location that's easy (and cheap) to get to. You could consider any of the areas of work mentioned later in this chapter. Jobs in these areas will be open to applicants who are school/college leavers and there will almost certainly be opportunities in your local area.

It may be tempting to look for the easiest or most convenient job you can, but try to prioritise vacancies by how much they pay. The difference between a job paying £6 per hour and one paying £6.50 might seem minimal, but over the course of a year, you could be looking at a difference in earnings of nearly £1,000.

To find a job you should look for vacancies in your local newspaper (or on their website) and on recruitment websites. Your local Jobcentre Plus office will have vacancies that may be suitable for you. There are also many gap year websites, some of which advertise jobs for gap-year students; the following are just a few examples of sites you could look at:

- www.yearoutwork.co.uk

- www.gapyearjobs.co.uk

- www.e4s.co.uk.

You could also think about signing up with a recruitment agency. To start earning as soon as possible, you could work as a 'temp' until something more long term becomes available. The important thing to remember is that you need to use your gap year to earn as much as possible, and the quicker you start working, the more you'll be able to earn.

There will be different kinds of work you could apply for, but aside from earning money, you may want a job that is relevant to your career and gives you the chance to gain valuable experience. If that's the case, you'll need to do some research.

Finding a job that's relevant to your career plans

If you are keen to find a job that is related to the subject you are planning to study and career you want in future, you could look for opportunities with relevant employers. There may be vacancies in support roles, which would be an option for you and would allow you to get a feel for the industry and perhaps make important contacts for the future. You could approach relevant employers 'on spec' or sign up with recruitment agencies that operate in the industry or sector you are interested in.

There are also a number of schemes that offer gap-year students paid work placements in businesses relevant to their area of study. One such scheme is The Year in Industry (YINI). YINI works with 300 UK companies to provide paid work placements to gap year students. Placements are available in the following areas:

- engineering

- science

- IT

- e-commerce

- business

- marketing

- finance and logistics.

Placements usually start around August/September and end the following July/August. Students are typically paid up to £14,000, although some earn more. During placements students have the chance to experience real business issues. For more information see: www.yini.org.uk.

The following website has links to the Step Classic and Step into Industry programmes. These programmes offer students the chance to take part in project-based placements, lasting between 8-12 weeks or sandwich placements lasting 6-12 months. Placements are advertised on: www.step.org.uk, along with details of how to apply.

If you can't find work that is relevant to your career

Although it's ideal to find a job that's relevant to your career, it's not always possible. Competition for all jobs can be fierce and there may not be many opportunities in your local area. If this is the case and you find yourself applying for any job that pays, don't worry. Any work you undertake will demonstrate to prospective employers and admissions tutors that you:

- are responsible and hardworking – full-time work isn't an easy option for anyone

- can work with other people

- have the capacity to learn new skills.

The important thing to remember is that any job you do during your gap year will help you earn much-needed cash, and the more you earn, the less you'll need to borrow.

Working part-time while you're at university – a good use of your time?

When you're at university you'll have to attend lectures, seminars, workshops etc and do your own independent study. But, as you'll discover, you may also have quite a lot of time to yourself. Of course, university isn't all about the work; you'll also want a social life. But if you want to reduce the amount of money you borrow, some of your time should be spent earning money!

The majority of students have to get a part-time job while they are studying to supplement their income. Not only will working earn you money, give you the chance to develop new skills and gain experience, it'll also save you money!

- The time you spend working will be time when you won't be able to go out spending money!

- The more you work, the less you'll have to borrow.

- Your job may even be able to save you money in other ways – especially if it has perks; this is explained later in this chapter.

How much time you'll be able to spend working will depend on your course. Obviously, doing well at university is important and you don't want to jeopardise your success by stretching yourself too thinly and not leaving enough time for study. Most courses, however, will allow you to balance study with paid employment. You will also be able to work during your university vacations, which can be lengthy.

During term time however, many universities advise their students not to commit to more than 15 hours of paid work a week. Ideally, it's worth looking for a job that has some flexibility; if you're able to vary your hours according to the changing demands of your course, your time will be much more manageable.

Is it worth it?

You may wonder whether it's even worth working if you can only commit to a few hours a week, but remember, **any** money you bring in will reduce the amount you have to borrow. For example, if you can work for ten hours a week, and you earn £5 an hour, that's £200 a month you'll be bringing in (or £2,400 a year!). It might not seem a fortune, but earning £2,000 is certainly better than owing £2,000.

Other ways of bringing in some cash

If you're not keen on finding a job while you're at university, you could investigate other ways of financing yourself.

- A **sponsored degree** course could pay your tuition fees and offer you the chance to get some useful work experience; for more details see Chapter two. Alternatively, you could think about learning while you earn through a Higher Apprenticeship or employer-funded study; these options are explained further in Chapter four.

- Completing a **paid placement** as part of your course is also a way of earning money at university. Many sandwich courses are available; these offer students the chance to get relevant, paid workplace experience as part of their time at university. For more information about sandwich degrees, see Chapter three.

- Working during **university vacations rather than during term time** is a good way of earning money if you don't fancy the idea of juggling the demands of your course with a job during the term. Many courses will require you to study or complete assignments over the Christmas and Easter breaks, but you probably won't be assigned any course work, apart from reading, over the summer months. This is an ideal time to find employment and many of the jobs described in this chapter will be open to you. Some typical student vacation jobs are listed later in this chapter.

Ideas for part-time jobs

You're at university and you want a job – so, what's available to you? There are lots of jobs that are suited to students; the areas and employers listed below are just some examples but might give you a few ideas.

- Retail work – clothes shops, supermarkets, gift shops, department stores, shoe shops, phone shops, newsagents, DIY stores, garden centres and petrol stations.

- Catering – restaurants, fast-food chains, cafés, sandwich shops and tea shops.

- Leisure – pubs and bars, cinemas, leisure centres, bowling alleys, casinos, nightclubs and theme parks.

- Hospitality – hotels, campsites and holiday parks.

These are all areas of work that students often find employment in. If you find a job in one of these areas, you may well be able to get extra hours during your university vacations. While you might not be keen to take any job, you should bear in mind that all jobs offer you the chance to gain experience and learn new skills. Even a part-time job could help you develop the following skills that a prospective employer will value.

Communication skills – dealing with customers and colleagues will improve your communication skills and may develop your confidence.

Teamwork skills – by working with other people you'll learn how to operate effectively in a team.

Problem–solving and initiative – whatever role you decide to take on, it's likely that you'll have to find ways to cope when problems arise – unhappy customers, late deliveries or faulty goods, for example. Working in a busy environment such as a restaurant or pub may mean you'll have to use your initiative to get a job done and keep customers happy.

Time-management – regardless of the job you take on, working part time will demonstrate to any future employer that you are capable of managing your own time and balancing work and study.

All these skills will look great on your CV. Your employer may well be able to give you a reference in the future as well. And, at the end of the day, even if it isn't your dream job, it will earn you money and help you avoid increasing your debt!

Jobs on campus

When you are looking for a job, one of the biggest employers you will come into contact with is your university. The benefits of working for your university are clear; not only will your workplace be easy to get to, but your employer will understand your study commitments. You may also find it's easier to juggle work with study as you'll be spending most of your time on campus. It's worth remembering though that these types of jobs may only be available during term time, so you would need to find another job for the vacations.

The variety of jobs at universities varies according to the size of the institution. Some campuses have sports centres, shops, cinemas and even arts centres, all of which need staff. All universities have student unions, which may recruit for some of the following roles.

Membership and events staff

Even small student unions run a variety of events throughout the year and all these require planning and a lot of work behind the scenes. Many universities recruit membership assistants to work in the union office and answer enquiries from students. Events staff are needed to set up equipment before a big night, put up posters, sell tickets and take money at the door.

Facilities staff

The student union bar is a popular place and you can get a job behind it rather than propping it up! As well as bar staff and glass collectors, there may also be vacancies for kitchen assistants and serving staff at student cafés and restaurants on campus. All universities offer some kind of accommodation on site, which needs to be cleaned on a regular basis. Sometimes this work is contracted out, but there are often vacancies for cleaning staff.

Library staff

Every university has a library and students are often employed to work alongside qualified librarians, re-stocking shelves, staffing the loans desk and carrying out basic administrative tasks.

Student ambassadors

The exact duties depend on the university, but in general a student ambassador's job is to promote the university. They may lead tours on open days, welcome new students, run revision workshops for school children, give presentations to sixth formers or visit local schools to promote higher education.

Wardens

Many universities employ student wardens who live in halls of residence and act as a first point of call for student with problems. The role might involve issuing keys to new students and taking inventories of items of furniture/kitchen equipment etc in each block. Some warden posts are paid and all posts usually include a generous accommodation package.

Fundraisers

Work is often available telephoning alumni (people who've graduated from the university in the past) to gather information on their careers since graduation and asking for donations towards campaigns the university is running, foundations for disadvantaged students or even areas of research.

Other opportunities

As well as working for the university itself, there are other ways to earn money on campus.

Campus brand managers, otherwise known as student brand managers and brand ambassadors, are employed by many organisations to promote their product, company or service to fellow students. The work varies according to the employer but may include representing the brand at student events, running promotional campaigns, liaising with student radio stations and magazines or advising the company on student behaviours and trends in the university. Companies that employ campus brand managers include: student travel companies, employers that run graduate recruitment programmes, publishers and manufacturers of products such as soft drinks. Most employers offer training and some even offer the opportunity to work towards a professional qualification in marketing. Pay varies but is often well above the National Minimum Wage; some positions also offer the chance to earn bonuses. Vacancies may be advertised through the job shop at your university (for more details see the end of the chapter).

If your university has a psychology department, it may be worth checking whether they ever look for **people to take part in research**. Many universities pay students to take part in psychology experiments – don't worry, these aren't medical trials but usually involve answering questions or taking part in simple tests, such as perception or memory tests. Some universities allow students to register with the psychology department so that they can be contacted whenever participants are needed. Pay varies; small experiments taking only 15 minutes or so may only pay £5-10 but more in depth studies may pay up to £60.

Jobs with perks

If you have a particular hobby or interest then it's worth trying to find a part-time job that can save you money by offering you perks you'd otherwise pay for. Lots of student jobs offer perks, even if it's just a discount off purchases, so there may well be something on offer that suits you.

Live music

If live music is your thing, check out jobs at music venues near you. If you can work at a venue, you'll be able to experience the buzz of live music without buying a ticket and while you're earning! Stewards are needed to check tickets and direct people to the right areas. There's also work available selling merchandise and serving behind bars.

You could look out for work at festivals; as well as stewards, bar staff etc, there may be work promoting particular products or handing out samples, directing traffic in car parks, giving out wristbands, picking up litter or staffing information points.

There are lots of useful websites that have information about part-time work in venues and at live events: www.festaff.co.uk lists job vacancies at festivals. See: www.efestivals.co.uk for a useful guide to working at festivals.

Films and theatre

If you're always keen on seeing the latest film release then you could look for work in your local cinema. Some of the large cinema chains offer employees cards that entitle them to free films, all year round – you may even get complimentary tickets for your friends. This could save you a lot of money if you're a regular cinema-goer!

Similarly, if you enjoy the theatre, then getting a job there could allow you to enjoy your passion and earn some cash! Part-time front of house positions may fit in with your studies, but competition for such roles is often great. You could also look for work at your local arts centre.

Sport and leisure

If keeping fit is important to you, try looking for jobs at your local sports centre. Depending on the facilities available, there may be work on reception, taking money from customers and handing out tickets, or as a leisure centre assistant, supervising the use of facilities, tidying away equipment and doing general housekeeping. If you've got the necessary qualifications you could work as a lifeguard at your local swimming pool. These sorts of jobs often offer free access to facilities, so this sort of work could save you the cost of a gym membership and earn you some money!

Shopping

Mystery shopping is a great way of earning money if you're a shopaholic. There are a number of agencies that specialise in mystery shopping and allow you to sign up, free of charge, as a shopper. When you have registered, you're then emailed details of jobs available. A job might involve buying an item from a specific store and then filling in a questionnaire about your experience. Pay varies, and isn't usually much – but lots of the assignments don't take huge amounts of time and you might be able to keep the item you've bought! Mystery shoppers are also employed to visit restaurants, bars etc which can mean a free meal or drink!

N.B You should be aware that although lots of people get involved in mystery shopping and enjoy it, there are some scams out there. Never part with any money to register with a company and be very wary of any 'jobs' promising to reimburse you if you purchase goods of high value; do your own research into any company you are interested in registering with.

Clubbing

Lots of students enjoy clubbing, but if you go regularly it can be costly. To earn some cash and get free entry to the clubs you like, try looking for work as a nightclub promoter. A club promoter's job is to get as many people as possible to their club, on the night they are working. They may walk around pubs in the area handing out flyers or free passes to students, or they might stand outside the club trying to attract people in. You need to be enthusiastic, confident and energetic for this type of work. Most club promoters are offered free entry and are paid according to the number of people they get through the door.

Job that use your skills

During your time at university you will be learning new skills. If you can find work that lets you use these skills you'll be able to earn money and gain experience at the same time. It can also help you compile a portfolio of your work, which will impress prospective employers in future.

The type of skills you have to offer will obviously affect the kind of work you're able to do, but if you're willing to think creatively, there may well be opportunities that you haven't considered before. Also, as this work may be more skilled than some of the usual part-time jobs on offer to students, you may well be able to earn more money.

Tutoring

If you're studying a subject that directly relates to school subjects (such as English, maths, science, humanities, music or a foreign language) you could consider tutoring. As well as school-aged children and young people, you may be able to find work teaching adults who want to learn a foreign language or musical instrument for pleasure, for instance.

You could advertise your services locally (perhaps on a website or through a college) or you could sign up to an agency. There are a number of agencies that look for tutors, some of whom may work online with students from all over the country. Tutoring is often quite well paid in comparison to other student jobs.

Website design and graphic design

If you have the skills there is work available in website design and graphic design (working on anything from flyers to logos). Not every business can afford to have a sophisticated bespoke website designed or invest in customised stationery and professionally-designed adverts. However if you are able to offer a good service at a reasonable price, you may well be of interest to small or new businesses. The biggest challenge facing any student who is interested in freelance work is finding customers. Obviously you won't have the money for big advertising campaigns, but for a very small fee you might be able to put up adverts in local shops or on local websites. The amount of money you could earn will depend on how much business you can get and how much you charge.

Other opportunities

Try to think about the skills you have already, and those that you will develop on your course. Could any of these skills earn you money?

More and more employers are realising that using students can be a great way to get specific projects done without employing someone full time or spending a lot on an experienced freelancer. Studentgems is a useful website that allows employers to advertise one-off, paid projects, which students can apply for. Students who register on the website can also build their own profile and advertise their skills; their profile is then added to the database, which employers can search. See: www.studentgems.com for more information.

Working during university vacations

University vacations – at Easter, Christmas and over the summer – are a great opportunity for you to earn money. Depending on your course, you may find that you have a few weeks at both Easter and Christmas and a couple of months over the summer when you're able to work more hours than you can during term time.

Many of the jobs and areas of work mentioned in this chapter are popular with students during vacations. If you are able to find a job during term time, your employer may well be able to offer you more hours during vacations. However, if your employer can't offer you extra hours, or your work is term-time only (such as jobs on campus) you could look out for seasonal opportunities for full-time work.

- Shops, bars and restaurants get very busy in the run up to Christmas and many employers take on extra staff just for this period.

- The summer brings a lot of seasonal work in areas popular with tourists – you may be able to find work in shops, cafés, bars, hotels or at tourist attractions.

- Royal Mail offers seasonal work in the run up to Christmas; staff may be employed to sort or deliver post.

- Organisations that run activity or holiday camps for children often look for staff during the summer, which is their busiest time.

- If you fancy working outside during the summer you could look into picking and packaging fruit and other crops.

- As summer is a busy time for events, such as festivals, weddings and fairs you may also be able to find work putting up marquees. Businesses that organise these types of events may also offer waitressing or promotional work.

Use the student jobs websites, listed below, to search for seasonal work.

How to find a job

There are lots of ways that you can find suitable work as a student.

- If you know who you want to work for, perhaps you want a job with a particular company or one that offers a certain perk, you can approach employers directly.

- Most universities have job shops – services that aim to find suitable part-time work for students. These services may advertise jobs on vacancy boards or websites; they may also run workshops on topics that will be relevant to you, such as organising your time and balancing work and study.

- Pay a visit to the student union office at your university as soon as you arrive to check out if there's any work available on campus.

- If you're interested in working as a campus brand manager, do some research on the internet. There are lots of companies on the lookout for new recruits – you could also ask about this type of work at your university job shop.

- There are many websites that list student jobs, including: www.justjobs4students.co.uk, www.student-jobs.co.uk, www.studentjob.co.uk, www.e4s.co.uk.

Final thoughts

Hopefully this chapter has opened your eyes to the many ways you can earn money before and during your degree. Working during a gap year is a popular way of saving money in advance of studying and this chapter has shown you how you can maximise your earning potential during that year. Earning doesn't have to stop when you start your course. If you're willing to do your research, you may be able to find something that saves you money on your hobbies, helps you build up a portfolio of work or even pays you a bit more than your local supermarket. Whether you are thinking of working throughout your course, or during a year out, think creatively and consider how you can put your skills to good use and earn the most during the time you have available.

Ask yourself...

- What type of job will earn you the most money?

- Would it be easier for you to work on campus?

- Which jobs could offer you money-saving perks?

- How can you use your skills to earn money?

Chapter eight

Find out, before you pay out!

As you will have discovered from the earlier chapters in this book, it makes sense to do as much research as you can before applying for university. You need to be sure that you've compared different universities, different courses and different modes of study so that you find the best option for you. There's a lot of information out there, so this chapter will help you:

- work out how to compare different courses

- find sources of information for UK courses

- find sources of information for overseas courses

- understand the standard types of financial support available and check whether you qualify for any additional support.

Comparing what's on offer

In total, UK universities offer around 50,000 full-time degree courses each year. Add in all the part-time, distance-learning and overseas courses available and it would be easy to feel overwhelmed with choices! Therefore, to find the best course for you, it may be easiest to take it in stages. Hopefully, having read the earlier chapters in this book with an open mind, you will have considered all the various options available and formed some opinions about which might work for you.

- Whatever your situation, there will be some options that just aren't feasible for you. Identify the things that you just can't compromise on, perhaps your degree subject, whether you study full or part time, whether you stay in the UK or go abroad, and so on. This will narrow down your options considerably.

- Then start thinking about the things that add most value to your degree experience. Refer back to Chapter one for a reminder of the employability factors and extracurricular activities that you should look for, to get more for your money. Filter out those courses that don't meet your requirements.

- This will leave you with a more manageable shortlist of courses that would all be acceptable to you – so you can now begin looking for the ones that work out cheapest overall.

It may help to sketch out a chart, so you can jot down, for each course, how much you will need to spend on fees, accommodation etc, as well as the potential bursaries and scholarships that will help offset the costs involved. Some costs won't vary much regardless of where you study, for example books and stationery, so concentrate on the things that differ depending on where you choose to study.

You may have to estimate some expenses, such as the cost of your daily commute, but at least you'll begin to get a sense of how these might impact on your overall outgoings. Make sure your calculations are based on comparable periods of time; for example, if you're looking at a three-year course, all the potential costs and income should relate to the entire three-year period.

Your chart might end up looking something like this:

COSTS THAT MAY VARY	Course 1	Course 2	Course 3	Etc.
Course fees				
Additional course costs (optional field trips, equipment etc)				
Accommodation				
Additional living expenses (food, utility bills etc – if not covered in accommodation costs)				
Travel – daily				
Travel – occasional (e.g. between university and home if moving away)				
Leisure activities (if they are likely to vary depending on location)				
Placement year costs (if applicable)				
TOTAL (A)				

INCOME THAT MAY VARY	Course 1	Course 2	Course 3	Etc.
Guaranteed bursaries/scholarships/grants				
Potential bursaries/scholarships/grants				
Earnings from working during term time				
Earnings from working during vacations				
Potential sponsorship				
Placement year earnings				
TOTAL (B)				
A – B				

By calculating the difference between the cost of each course and any income you earn while you study (A – B), you will be able to see which courses are likely to work out cheapest for you.

N.B. To work out how much you will have to borrow in total to finance your higher education, remember to factor in any other costs and income that are deliberately excluded from your previous calculations. For example, the costs of books are unlikely to vary between different courses but would need to be accounted for. Likewise, remember to include any savings you may already have or expect to earn from a gap year, plus any financial support you may get from your parents etc.

The following sections will point you in the direction of where you can find out the necessary information in order to complete your comparisons.

UK courses

The starting point for any research about full-time courses undertaken in the UK has to be through **UCAS**, the organisation responsible for managing higher education applications to universities, colleges and some music conservatoires. There's a great deal of information to be found on the UCAS website, www.ucas.com. As well as general advice and guidance about the application process and student finance, UCAS provides information about individual courses and universities including details on course fees, bursaries and scholarships, accommodation and much more. The UCAS website also links to the websites of individual universities, making it easy to find more detailed information where necessary.

To find out details about part-time and distance-learning courses, you will have to refer directly to each university or provider that interests you, as these are not included in the UCAS listings. Chapter four has details of the major providers. Alternatively, the **Hotcourses** website, www.hotcourses.com, offers a useful way of searching for part-time and distance-learning courses.

Another means of comparing individual universities and courses all in one place is through the **Unistats** website, www.unistats.com, a publicly funded service that aims to help students make informed choices about their higher education. Here you will find results from the annual **National Student Survey**, which gathers feedback from undergraduates in their final year of study at all publicly funded higher education institutions in England, Wales, Northern Ireland and Scotland. All further education colleges in England that provide higher education courses also participate in the survey, as does the University of Buckingham (a private university). The Unistats site also brings together other useful information from various official sources.

The following sections of this chapter point out where you can research some of the main factors that will affect the cost and value of courses that interest to you, relating to:

- accommodation costs
- bursaries, scholarships, awards and other financial support
- course fees
- employability
- financial support
- general statistics about each institution
- student satisfaction
- travel costs.

Accommodation costs

As Chapter five has already described, your accommodation costs are obviously a major consideration when choosing where to study. UCAS offers a good starting point for investigating how accommodation costs can vary, by listing the estimated weekly cost of institution-managed accommodation. The UCAS website also provides links to each university's website for further information.

As well as information about the accommodation costs for their own managed properties, most universities will also provide an estimate of rents in the private sector, for example, the cost of sharing a private house with other students. Obviously, it's also incredibly simple to conduct your own internet research and check out likely costs through private rental agencies specialising in student lets.

Bursaries, scholarships, awards and other financial support

Finding out what's available

You can find out about university scholarships, bursaries and awards from a number of sources; these are summarised below. Chapter two provides further details of these, as well as some other commercial directories and websites.

- Individual universities publish full details about the range of financial assistance they offer.

- The UCAS website allows you to compare the potential bursaries and scholarships available for up to six different courses at once.

- The Office for Fair Access (OFFA) holds details of access agreements from each university; these set out in full the fees, scholarship schemes, bursaries and so on that relate to the given university. The website, www.offa.org.uk, provides a search facility for access agreements.

A summary of the standard financial support, i.e. loans and grants, that you can expect to receive is given later in this chapter.

To get an estimate of the total amount of financial support you are entitled to, including student loans, grants, scholarships and bursaries, there are various online finance calculators you can use. Financial support varies according to where you live in the UK and where you plan to study. If you normally live in:

- England - visit the Directgov website, www.direct.gov.uk, and search for 'student finance calculator'

- Wales - visit the Student Finance Wales website: www.studentfinancewales.co.uk

- Scotland - visit the website of the Student Awards Agency for Scotland: www.saas.gov.uk

- Northern Ireland – visit the Student Finance Northern Ireland website: www.studentfinanceni.co.uk.

The National Scholarship Programme

The National Scholarship Programme (NSP) will apply to students starting at an English university in autumn 2012 and beyond. If you are eligible, your university will offer you benefits worth at least £3,000 in your first year of study (and a pro-rata amount for part-time students); Chapter two has further details. To find out whether you qualify for an NSP award and how this might benefit you, you will need to check the website of the university you are interested in; the UCAS website will provide quick links for you to access the relevant information.

Course fees

Chapter five gives an overview of the different fee arrangements for full-time courses depending on where you live and study in the UK. For exact fees for individual full-time courses, visit the UCAS website; this may be the quickest way of comparing different courses in the first instance. Obviously, individual universities also publish their fees in their prospectuses and on their websites.

In due course, it is likely that a number of independent organisations will set up comparison websites or other types of directory that will allow you to quickly and easily compare the tuition fees for different courses. Make sure you only use reputable sites and that you check how up to date the information is.

Employability

For most people, improving their career prospects is the main motivation for gaining a degree. Therefore, it makes sense to check whether the courses that interest you are likely to lead to meaningful employment.

By subject

Chapter one has already described how your choice of subject can impact on your employability. For an idea of the type of work graduates go into each year according to their degree subject, there's an annual report called *What Do Graduates Do?* This shows employment rates and typical occupations of UK graduates by subject, six months after graduation. The report (compiled by the Higher Education Careers Service Unit and the Association of Graduate Careers Advisory Services, in association with

UCAS) is available to download from the Graduate Prospects website, www.prospects.ac.uk.

By course

Once you have selected the degree subject that you wish to study, you will still find that some universities have better employability rates for their students than others. This may be for a number of reasons, including:

- how prestigious the university is perceived to be
- how many links the university has developed with potential employers
- the quality of the university's careers service
- how much importance the university places on developing its students employability skills
- the enrichment opportunities available to students, such as the extracurricular activities, optional extras and so on, described in more detail in Chapter one.

To gain the most value from your degree course, it makes sense, therefore, to choose one that maximises your chances of gaining a relevant, graduate-level job at the end of your studies. The Unistats website provides useful statistics on the percentage of students who are working in a graduate job six months after completing each course, as well as the type of professions entered.

General statistics about each institution

When it comes to choosing between different universities or courses, there are some factors that have no obvious costs, but are still worth considering. For example, knowing about the type of students who attend an institution won't affect how much you need to pay, but may impact on your overall enjoyment of the course and your motivation to see it through to the end.

You may feel that you will get the most out of your university experience if you 'fit in' with the other students around you. Alternatively, it may be important that you have the opportunity to study alongside a more diverse group of people. In either case, so long as your course provides you with what you are looking for, then your money will have been well spent.

If these are significant considerations for you, make sure you check the student profiles for each university. UCAS supplies statistics about each university as a whole, while Unistats gives similar statistics for each university broken down to subject level. The types of statistics available include the:

- overall number of students at each university/by subject area
- percentage of mature students
- percentage of international students
- ratio of male to female students
- ratio of full-time to part-time students.

UCAS also reports on the number of current students who are on a work placement or study period abroad, which may give you some indication as to how well supported such options are at your chosen university.

Student satisfaction

To get the most value from your investment in higher education, it's important that you see the course successfully through to graduation, achieving the best academic result you possibly can. It's very hard to predict how well you will get on with your studies or what standard of teaching you will receive for your money, but one way may be to see how previous students have rated each course. You can find overall satisfaction rates for each course via the UCAS website. The rates given come from the National Student Survey. Visit the Unistats website for a full breakdown of results from the latest survey; here you will find student feedback on:

- quality of teaching
- assessment and feedback
- academic support
- organisation and management
- learning resources
- personal development
- overall satisfaction.

The Unistats website also gives statistics on the numbers of students who didn't progress after the first year of their studies. Look out for courses with relatively high proportions of students who left after the first year, as this might be a cause for concern and require further investigation.

You will find there's plenty more information available if you want to dig deeper and get a better sense of what each course or university might be like.

- Each **university** publishes course information, usually outlining which topics you will study on the course, as well as how you will be taught and assessed. Check prospectuses or university websites to make sure that you know what to expect. You may also find testimonials from other students, which may give you some flavour of the course. These may be useful, but remember, universities are only likely to include positive testimonials about themselves! Attending university open days is critical if you want to get a feel for what each university is really like or if you have any specific questions about courses.

- There are various independent '**league tables**' that rank universities – giving you some idea about the quality of teaching, student/staff ratios, entry standards, completion rates, investment in facilities, degree results, employment prospects and so on. Look out for such tables published by the *Times Higher Education (THE)* magazine, as well as by *The Times, The Sunday Times, The Independent* and *Guardian* newspapers, among others.

It's worth taking the time to do this type of investigation. You may be surprised to find that some of the older, more established universities don't score highly across all factors relating to student satisfaction. In contrast, some of the institutions that became established as universities more recently may not rank highly overall, but students may have rated them better than average in particular areas, such as quality of teaching.

When it comes to trying to work out which courses and universities offer you best value for money, only you can decide how important it is for you to attend what might be perceived as a prestigious university compared with how likely you are to be satisfied with the course.

Travel costs

The costs involved in travelling to and from university on a daily basis, as well as the occasional costs of going back to the family home if you move away, will obviously vary depending on the location of your chosen university. The quickest and easiest way of finding out which universities are in the best location for you is to check the UCAS universities and colleges map. The map on the UCAS website is interactive, making it particularly useful when researching your options.

For each university, UCAS lists details of the campus locations and associated colleges. Make sure you find out whether your chosen university operates out of a single site or whether it has two or more campuses. This is important because, depending on your subject choice, you may find that you have to commute between different sites on a regular basis, or be based out in a smaller campus with fewer facilities or even in a completely different town to the main university site. All of which may have financial implications that you need to consider.

Overseas courses

If you are considering studying abroad, unfortunately, there's no quick, one-stop source of information; you will need to do a bit more digging around than for UK-based courses. As described in Chapter six, a good starting point is always the embassy or high commission of the country you wish to study in. Most have information for international students on their websites.

General information and advice is available from UKCISA (the UK Council for International Student Affairs). You can find out more from their website, www.ukcisa.org.uk, or by phoning their student advice line, tel: 0207 107 9922.

Just as with UK universities, there are various international league tables, which might prove useful if you want to feel confident that you are going to a well-respected institution. One such league table is published by the *THE* and can be viewed at:
www.timeshighereducation.co.uk/world-university-rankings.

Standard funding

The main aim of this book is to show you that you have options when it comes to higher education. By researching those options carefully, you will be able to find ways of gaining a degree that cost less than others or give you better value for money. However, you may still have to borrow money to fund your studies. Before you can calculate how much you'll need to borrow, you'll need to know what standard funding is available to you.

The precise amount you are entitled to varies from year to year and according to factors such as:

- which part of the UK you come from

- whether you plan to study full or part time

- whether you live at home or not

- whether you live in London or elsewhere (if you live away from home)

- your household income (for some types of funding)

- the length of your course

- which year of study you are applying for (e.g. some payments vary for your final year of study)

- your age.

You should therefore check official sources to find out exactly what you are entitled to.

The websites of the student finance organisations for England, Wales, Northern Ireland and Scotland are listed earlier in this chapter and tell you all you need to know about funding arrangements for your particular circumstances.

Summary of standard funding available

As a simplified guide, the typical funding available for full-time and part-time students is summarised in the following table. For each type of financial support, the table shows whether you will need to repay the amount at a later date and whether the amount you receive varies according to your household income.

Be aware that all funding arrangements may be subject to change over time, depending on Government policy.

Type of funding	Repayable?	Income assessed?	Available to full-time students?	Available to part-time students?
Tuition fee loan A payment made directly to your university on your behalf to pay for your course fees.	Yes	No	Yes	*
Living cost loan Money lent to you to cover your day-to-day living expenses. Known as a Maintenance Loan in England and Wales.	Yes	Yes	Yes	No
Living cost grant Money paid to you to help cover your day-to-day living expenses. Known as a Maintenance Grant in England and Northern Ireland, and as the Assembly Learning Grant in Wales. In Scotland, a range of bursaries is available for a similar purpose. For those who are in receipt of certain types of benefits, the Special Support Grant replaces other types of living cost grants.	No	Yes	Yes	No
Fee grant * Money to help pay your tuition fees.	No	Yes	No	Yes
Course grant * Money to help towards your study costs, such as books, materials and travel.	No	Yes	No	Yes

* In England, tuition fee loans will be available for part-time students who meet eligibility criteria, starting courses from September 2012 onwards.

** In England, course grants and fee grants will not be available for students starting part-time courses after the end of the 2011/12 academic year.

Additional support for special cases

You may find you qualify for extra financial support due to your personal circumstances. Often, the money available is to ensure that you are not at a disadvantage due to circumstances beyond your control. So while it is definitely worth checking what you might be entitled to, remember that any support you claim may simply help put you on an equal footing with other students around you, rather than save you money.

Charitable trusts, in particular, may offer loans or non-repayable grants to underrepresented groups such as women, people from ethnic minority groups or those from disadvantaged backgrounds. See Chapter two for more information.

Students in hardship

If you find yourself in particular hardship once you've started a course, you may be able to apply for extra help from your university. Funds are available for universities to pay out at their discretion if you need help with, for example:

- everyday living costs
- support during the vacations
- a financial crisis or exceptional financial cost
- other financial problems that may affect your ability to continue with your course.

Universities decide their own rules on eligibility – they may prioritise certain groups of people, such as lone parents, care leavers, final-year students and so on. They also decide in what way they will support you – either through a loan or non-repayable grant, through a one-off payment or in instalments, etc.

The funds go by different names, depending on where you study in the UK:

- Access to Learning Funds in England
- Support Funds in Northern Ireland
- Financial Contingency Funds in Wales
- Discretionary Funds in Scotland.

The Directory of Social Change publishes both *The Guide to Educational Grants*, which lists sources of non-statutory help for students in financial need, and *The Guide to Grants for Individuals in Need*, which lists sources of non-statutory help for the relief of individual poverty – look out for up-to-date copies in your local library.

Students with disabilities

There's a range of additional support available if you are a student with a disability (which includes ongoing health conditions, mental health conditions and specific learning difficulties, such as dyslexia). One of the best sources of information is the Directgov website, www.direct.gov.uk, where you will find details of:

- Disabled Students' Allowance – non-repayable grants to help cover the extra costs that arise through having a disability

- Disability Living Allowance – a tax-free benefit to help cover the costs if you need help with your personal care or with getting around

- Employment and Support Allowance/Incapacity Benefit – if you already claim either of these benefits, you may be able to continue claiming them as a student (the Employment and Support Allowance replaced Incapacity Benefits for new claimants from October 2008 onwards).

Students with dependants

If you are a parent undertaking a full-time course, you may be entitled to additional financial support, depending on your circumstances. For example, you may receive help with the cost of childcare or course costs. Visit the Directgov website for further information about:

- Childcare Grants

- Parents' Learning Allowance

- Child Tax Credits

- income-related benefits that may be available to lone parents or to couples, with responsibility for a child, who are both students.

As a full-time student, you are also entitled to a grant if you have an adult (typically, a member of your family, but not grown-up sons or daughters) who is dependent on you financially. The Directgov website has further details about the Adult Dependants' Grant.

Students on low incomes

You may be entitled to a range of state benefits depending on your situation. For example, you may be able to claim:

- income-related benefits such as Income Support, Housing Benefit and Council Tax Benefit

- Jobseeker's Allowance

- Working Tax Credit.

The eligibility rules are complex and, depending on the particular benefit you are claiming, will take into account factors such as whether you are a full- or part-time student, your income, your savings, whether you are a lone parent, your availability for work, your age and so on. The Directgov website has more information. If you already receive benefits and want to find out how becoming a student will affect your entitlement, seek advice from the appropriate authorities, such as the Jobcentre Plus or local authority Housing Benefit section.

Final thoughts

Investigating the costs of different courses and the various ways you can boost your income while you study will take time and effort. Make sure you allow yourself enough time to thoroughly research your options and to seek advice before you start applying for courses. Teachers, careers advisers and university admissions staff are there to offer information, advice and guidance, so make good use of them!

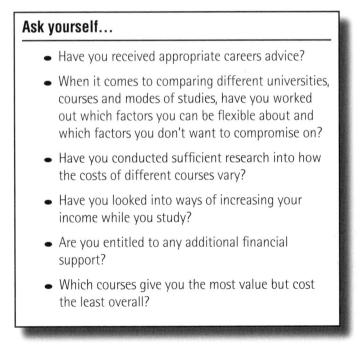

Ask yourself...

- Have you received appropriate careers advice?

- When it comes to comparing different universities, courses and modes of studies, have you worked out which factors you can be flexible about and which factors you don't want to compromise on?

- Have you conducted sufficient research into how the costs of different courses vary?

- Have you looked into ways of increasing your income while you study?

- Are you entitled to any additional financial support?

- Which courses give you the most value but cost the least overall?

This book has introduced you to the many different factors that impact on the cost of a degree. Knowing that some options can work out cheaper than others means that you should now be able to assess which courses offer you the best value for money and enable you to achieve a degree with less debt. Good luck!

Index

Other titles in this series...

The Student Helpbook series from Lifetime Publishing aims to help students of all ages make the right choices about their careers and education.

To view our full range of resources, visit: www.lifetime-publishing.co.uk.

A Year Off... A Year On? – Making the most of your gap year

This book contains practical, impartial advice about travelling, volunteering or working, as well as details of over 250 organisations offering opportunities to gap-year students.

8th edition   £11.99   ISBN: 978-1-902876-86-3

Careers with a Science Degree – Over 100 job ideas to inspire you

An invaluable resource for anyone who wants to know where a science degree could lead. Over 100 jobs are described, including entry requirements and training information.

5th edition   £12.99   ISBN: 978-1-904979-39-5

Careers with an Arts or Humanities Degree – Over 100 job ideas to inspire you

An invaluable resource for anyone who wants to know where an arts or humanities degree could lead. Over 100 jobs are described, including entry requirements and training information.

5th edition   £12.99   ISBN: 978-1-904979-40-1

CVs and Applications – A beginner's guide

Aimed at young people who want to know how to write their first CV or apply for their first job, this easy-to-use guide explains all! It includes tips on finding opportunities, understanding what selectors look for, understanding what you have to offer, presenting yourself effectively on paper or online, keeping track of applications – and much more!

7th edition   £12.99   ISBN: 978-1-904979-44-9

Decisions at 13/14+ – A guide to all your options

Aimed at Year 9 students, this book describes the GCSE and Diploma subjects available and includes a comprehensive careers guide covering over 130 different jobs.

11th edition   £11.99   ISBN: 978-1-904979-13-5

Decisions at 15/16+ – A guide to all your options

A comprehensive guide for students choosing their post-16 options. This book includes information on different types of qualifications and training opportunities, where to study and how to apply.

12th edition   £12.99   ISBN: 978-1-904979-45-6

Decisions at 17/18+ – A guide to all your options

This book covers all the major routes available to students who have gained level 3 qualifications, including higher education, work with training and taking a gap year.

6th edition   £11.99   ISBN: 978-1-902876-94-8

Excel at Interviews – Tactics for job and college applicants

Packed with case studies, quotes, examples and activities, this useful book includes clear, impartial advice on everything students need to know in order to successfully prepare for their first interview.

6th edition   £11.99   ISBN: 978-1-904979-22-7

Jobs and Careers after A levels and equivalent advanced qualifications

As well as describing the opportunities that are available for students leaving school or college at 18, this book includes advice on job-hunting, applications and interviews. Career profiles of 40 young people working in a diverse range of occupations provide an engaging insight into the alternative to higher education.

9th edition   £11.99   ISBN: 978-1-904979-21-0

Student Life: A Survival Guide – Practical advice & help with starting life at university

For anyone about to start university or college, this book offers practical advice on where to live, settling in, managing money, making friends, staying healthy and much more.

4th edition   £11.99   ISBN: 978-1-904979-01-2

Which A levels? – The guide to choosing A levels, Advanced Diplomas and other post-16 qualifications

This popular, student-friendly guide features over 50 AS/A level subjects and the range of Advanced Diplomas, as well as providing an overview of other post-16 qualifications. It includes the career and higher education options that are available following the courses described.

7th edition   £14.99   ISBN: 978-1-904979-41-8